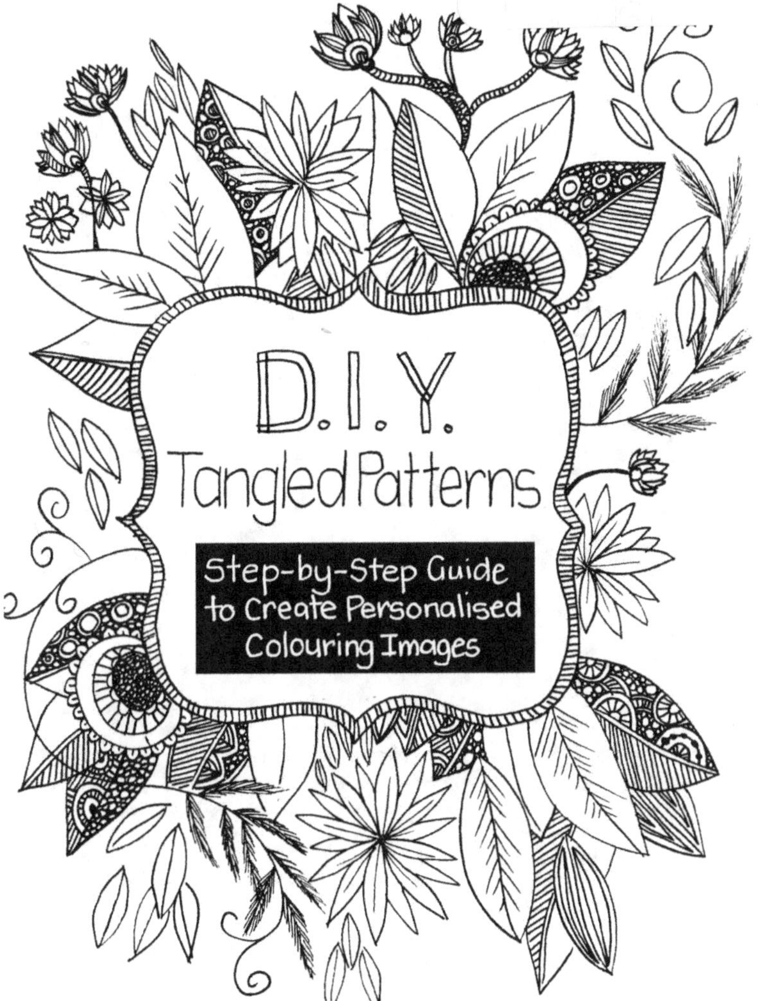

D. I. Y.

Tangled Patterns

Step-by-Step Guide
to Create Personalised
Colouring Images

DB DYANBURGESS

Foreword

Creating art has always been a part of who I am. However, with four children, it became difficult to find the time.

So a few years ago, I experimented with the idea of carrying a small Moleskine notebook, with the plan to draw whenever I had a spare moment.

Thankfully the idea worked even better than expected, and before long I'd built up a collection of illustrations, including many that were suitable for colouring later on.

I discovered that 'doodling' on the go was an extremely practical and rewarding way to create meaningful art.

This book is my way of sharing this simple pleasure with others.

I hope that my step-by-step instructions, examples, tips and stories will help you to bring your own pictures to life.

Practice Here

Contents

Practice Here

Colouring Books
vs.
Tangled Patterns

Many of us have been introduced to the beauty of tangled patterns through the colouring book craze.

But have you ever stopped to think about the wonder of tangled patterns as artworks in their own right, not merely as something to be coloured in?

And have you ever considered that you could get so much more enjoyment by creating your own meaningful patterns to later colour in?

You could be a tangler as well as a colourer.

This book is designed to show you how.

So get ready to start creating beautiful images...

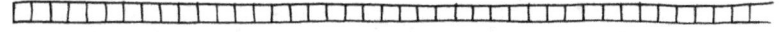

A bit more about colouring books

Why are adult colouring books so popular right now?

It seems that adults have embraced the opportunity to return to their childhoods, get away from their screens, and become immersed in the meditative process of colouring.

So with colouring books popping up everywhere from the two dollars stores to high-end retailers, why would we want to print another one?

Well, this book is a bit different.

The aim of this book is to help you to create your own images for colouring.

That way you get the creative benefits of creating the image, as well as colouring it.

And you can complete one project at a time rather than have endless unfinished colouring books lying around your home.

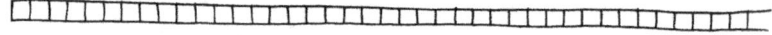

Zentangle vs. Doodle vs. Tangled Patterns

There are several different terms used for the intricate line drawings we see in many colouring books.

Zentangle (www.zentangle.com) is a proprietary name for a particular practice of drawing patterns.

The focus of these drawings is to let your mind relax while consciously drawing structured patterns. A bit like yoga for your mind.

Doodle is an American term usually referring to a more absent-minded scribbling or drawing. The term is also used in Australia but, beware, it can also mean something quite different.

Tangled patterns or *tangles* are my preferred terms and represent a more mindful approach than simply doodling.

I also like that the terms can be likened to the metaphorical tangles that we sometimes experience in our lives.

As you transfer the tangles onto paper, perhaps this book can help you become a little less tangled in your everyday life.

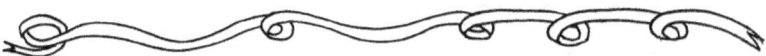

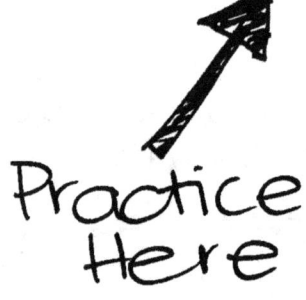

Practice
Here

How to use this book

The structure of this book is as follows:

Part 1:

This part provides three examples including images with detailed step-by-step instructions about how they were created.

Part 2:

This part is divided into five chapters each focusing on a particular theme.

Within each chapter there is:

- a story about the image
- a picture of the image
- templates for you to create your own story and image
- additional space for your notes.

Setting up the book in this way allows you to keep your thoughts and ideas in order so you can create images at your own pace, whenever the urge takes you.

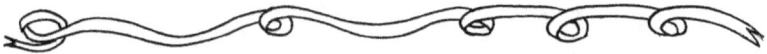

Practice
Here

What you need to get started...

HB pencil or mechanical pencil

My preference is the 0.5 mm mechanical pencil with HB refills.

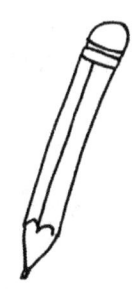

Waterproof ink pens

If using pen, it's important that you use waterproof to avoid smudging.

Pens can range from 0.005 to 2.0.

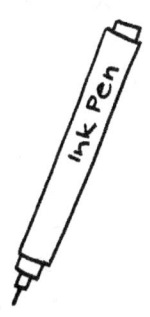

For beginners it's useful to have a range of line sizes, say 0.1, 0.3, 0.4 and 0.5 pens.

However, if you can only choose one pen, I'd recommend the 0.4 size.

Currently my brand of choice is Unipin as they are readily available at most stores and don't tend to bleed on planes (very messy story there!).

If you know that you will be copying or scanning your images, test how the different pens work for your copier or scanner.

Usually, the smaller sizes – 0.005 and 0.01 – can become difficult to see. However, it depends on the machine that you are using and the ultimate result that you want.

Moleskine notebook

My personal preference is the Evernote grid version. The faint grid lines help me draw straight but disappear when I copy or scan the image.

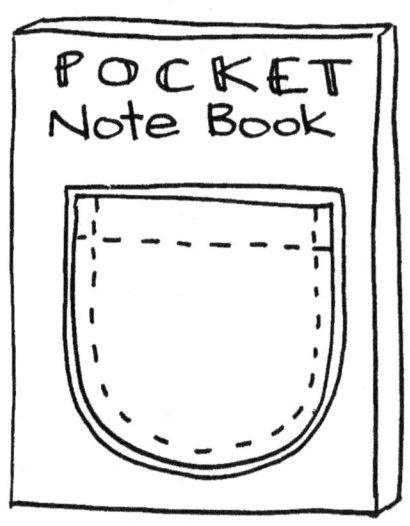

The small pocket-size Moleskine is great for carrying around in a zip lock sandwich bag along with a pen. Then, when you have a few minutes, waiting in queues, or in between appointments, you can quickly note down your thoughts or build on an image.

This book

This book has been designed to give you all the inspiration you need to get started. It's also small enough to carry in your bag so you can make notes and build up your images on the go.

Practice Here

Practice Here ↓

Tips to get started...

Relax:

Remember, the purpose of both colouring and tangling is the same; to encourage you to relax and take the time to be present with yourself.

Breathe:

First, take a deep breath in through your nose while counting to seven. Hold for seven. Breath out for nine counts.

Repeat four times.

NOTE: This breathing technique can be uncomfortable the first time you do it. However, soon it will become effortless and your body with thank you.

You can use this technique any time or place to relax your body and mind.

Now you are ready to continue.

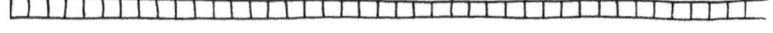

Look around

Take your time to look at the world around you.

Look at the shapes. Take note of the lines.

Are they straight?

Are they curved?

What do you feel when you see these lines?

Think about those lines when you pick up your pen or pencil to draw.

Use those feelings to guide your choice of lines when you draw.

What do you like about them?

Does it make you feel happy?

Does it remind you of something you like?

Sketch it out

When drawing patterns, you may want to sketch with pencil first and then ink over the final lines.

This is a matter of personal preference.

Sometimes I like the challenge of working purely with ink, knowing that I cannot rub it out and seeing where this takes me.

Other times, when I have a more set idea about what I want to achieve, I do a pencil image first.

Another idea is to use tracing paper to trace over your patterns so you can test out different results.

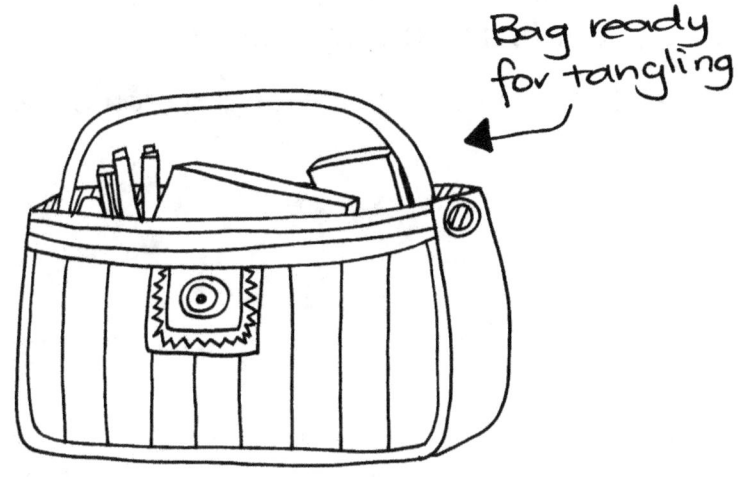

Bag ready for tangling

Taking it a step further

If you're already familiar with tangling and the colouring craze, perhaps this book will provide you with a new perspective of your craft and challenge you to approach your images in a new way.

Maybe you'll even be inspired to create a book of your own images to share with others.

Free templates

To assist with your practice of tangling I have provided free templates at:

 www.dyanburgess.com/freetangling_templates

Enjoy!

PART 1

Practice
Here

STEP-by-STEP

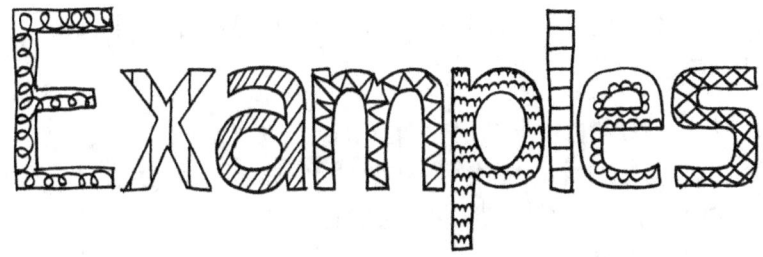
Examples

Here are three step-by-step patterns to give you an idea of how to get started.

There are no hard and fast rules as to how these images develop or how they should look. The idea is to gain your own style over time.

In the examples, no particular plan was set out beforehand. Pen was put to paper to see what would develop.

Relax. Breathe. Draw. Enjoy.

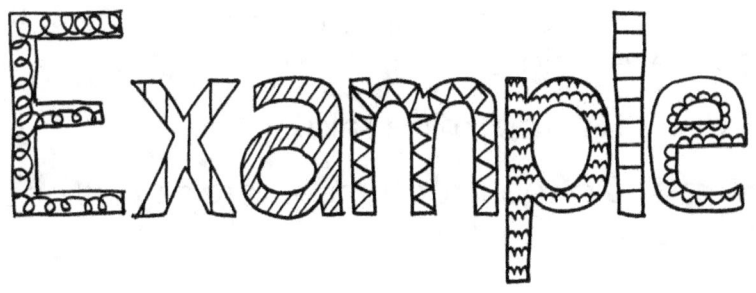

ONE

TANGLED PATTERN

Like most activities, making a tangled pattern can be broken down into a relatively simple process that can be repeated and refined.

In this first example, to get you started, I have outlined very detailed steps so you can easily immerse yourself in the process.

The subsequent examples are shorter with a little less detail.

Step 1: Let your mind relax.

Step 2: Do the breathing exercise outlined on page xvii.

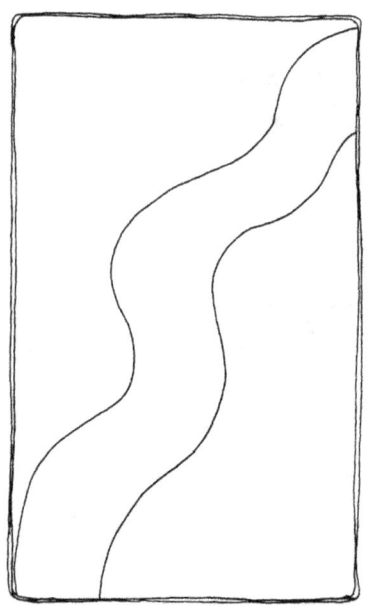

Step 3: Pick up your pen and notebook. In this example I am working with a 0.5 Unipin so it is easier to see the details.

Step 4: Choose a shape or line. In this example, I start with two wavy lines.

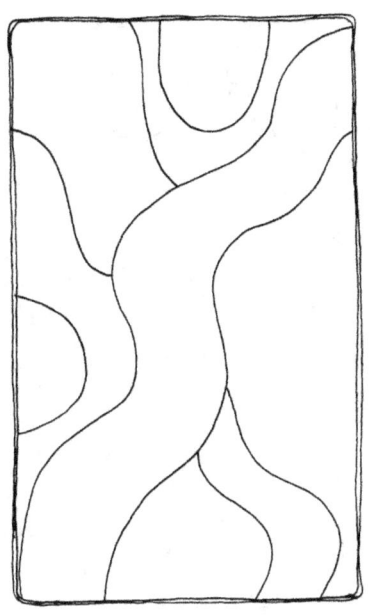

Step 5: Continue to add large shapes and lines.

Step 6: Add more lines and shapes to give more structure to work on. The simplest way to get a balanced pattern is to use the existing lines and repeat.

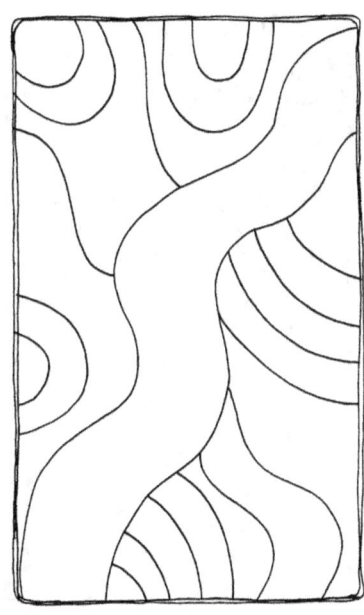

Step 7: Choose an area and start to add more detailed patterns. Remember, you can turn your page any way you like so you feel comfortable with your drawing.

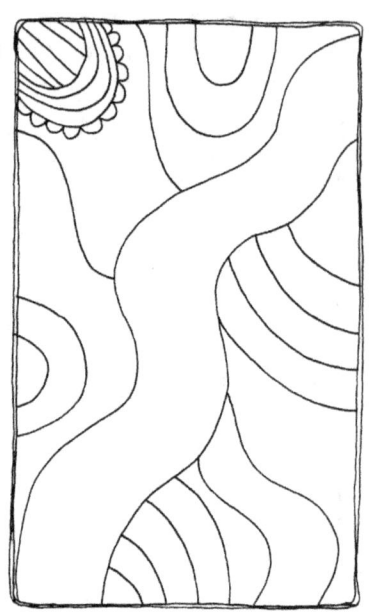

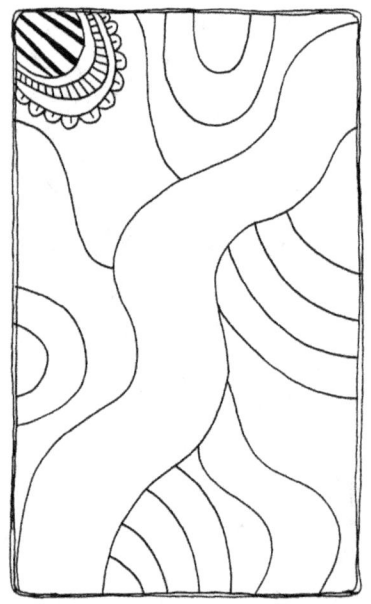

Step 8: Continue to add detail to the small shapes you have created.

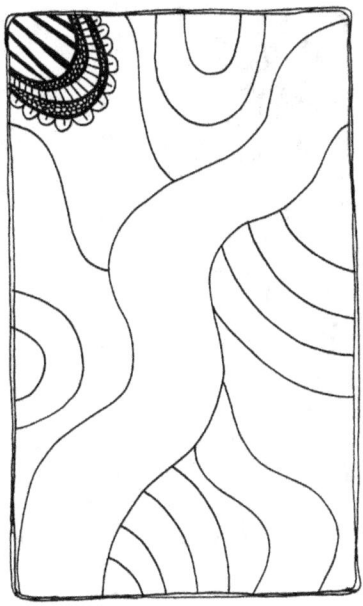

Step 9: You can fill in some of the detail.

Step 10: Expand your pattern into the next area.

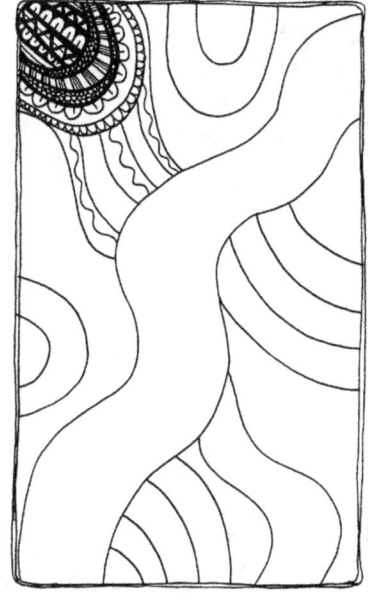

Step 11: Review what lines you have done so far. Use them in the extension of your pattern.

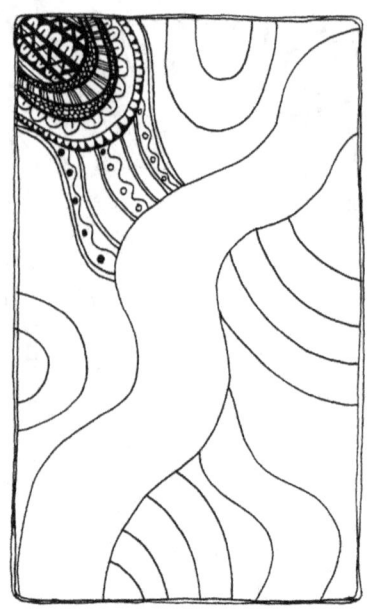

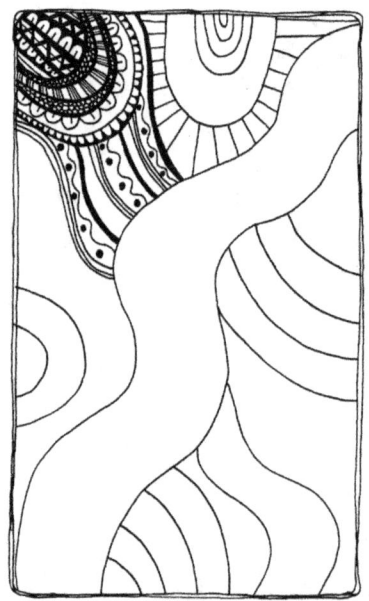

Step 12: Develop the next area.

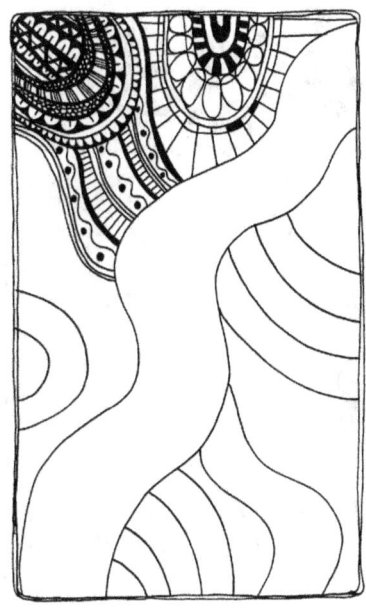

Step 13: Work on the detail.

Step 14: Fill in the detail.

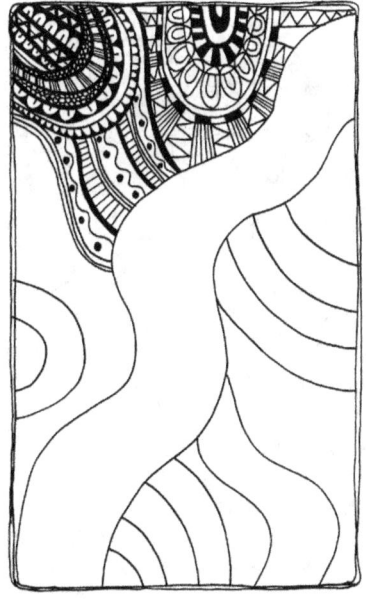

Step 15: Refine and continue to fill the detail.

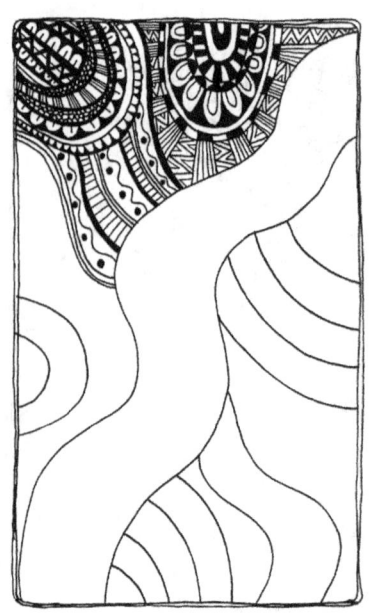

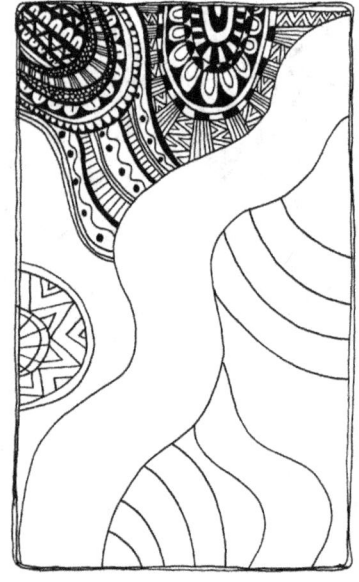

Step 16: Start a new area.

And so on...

Draw larger lines.

Put detail into the section.

Fill in space.

How much solid black you use may depend on whether you intend to colour the image or leave it as a line drawing. In the rest of this pattern, you can see that I've left more open space, which would be better suited to colouring.

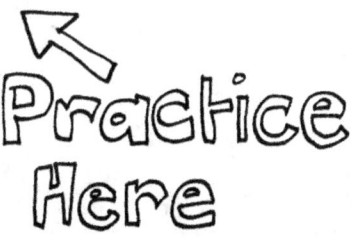

Practice Here

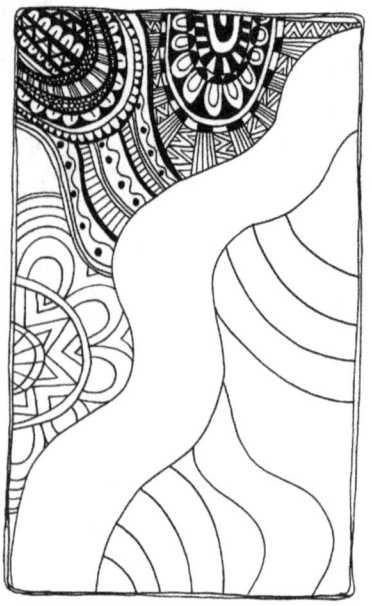
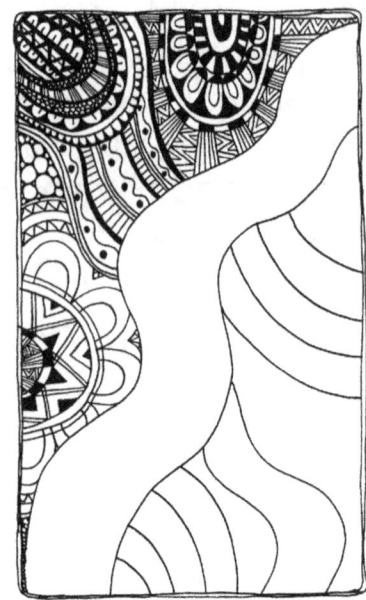
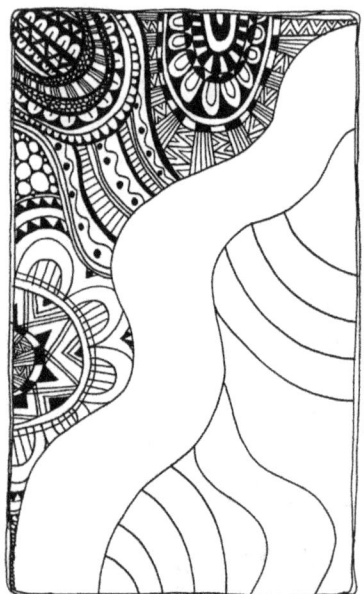
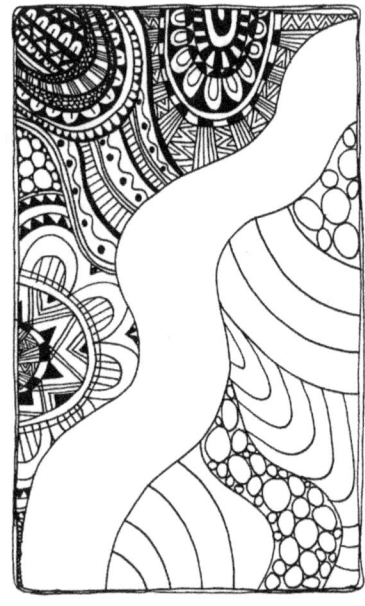

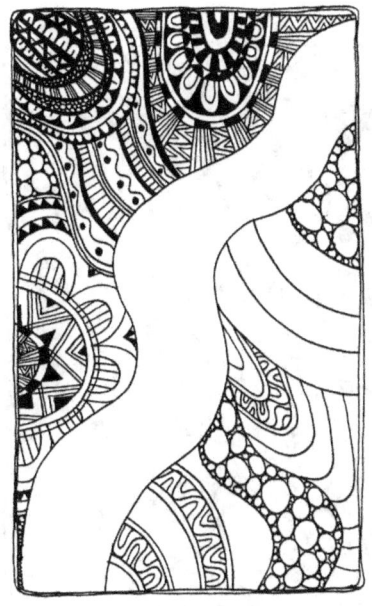
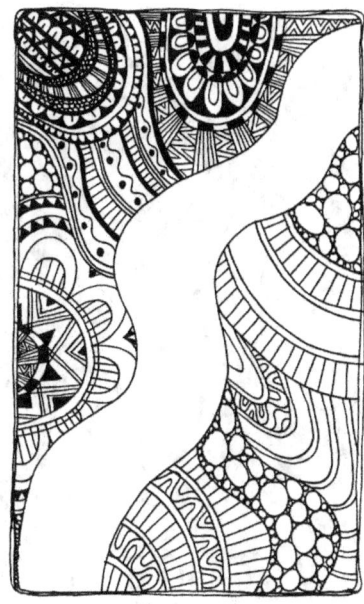
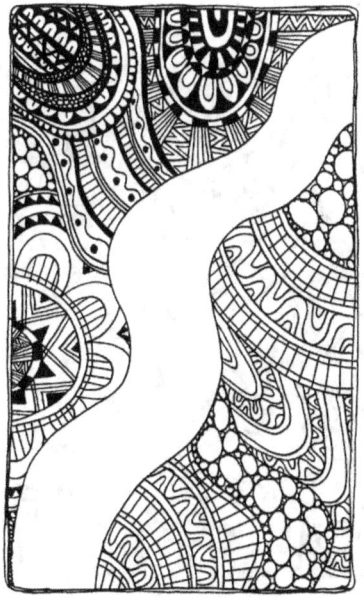
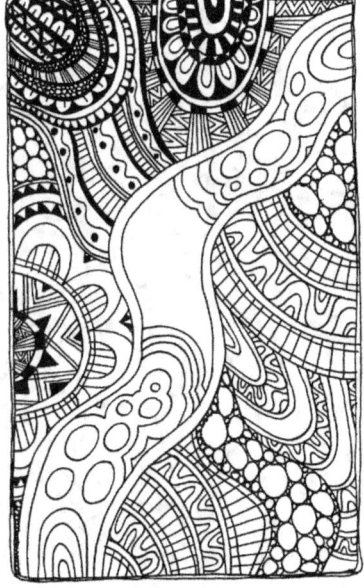

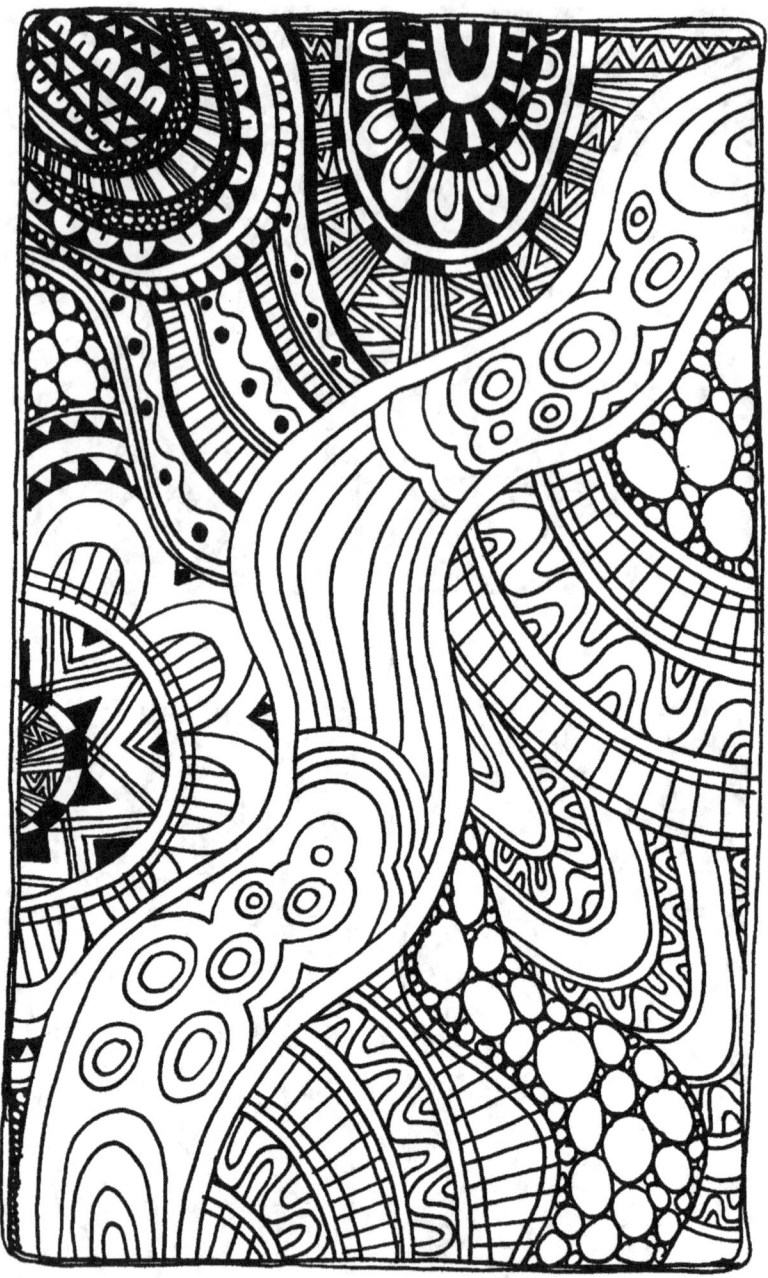

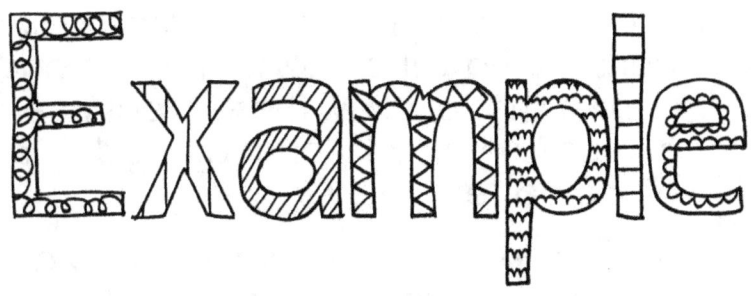

TWO

REPEAT PATTERN

This example uses a quarter circle template, to demonstrate how to create a repeat pattern.

With a repeat pattern you simply create part of the pattern and then repeat it to create a symmetrical image (see more details in Chapter 3 page 77).

When developing your design, make sure you consider how the image meets along the straight lines or axes. These areas need to be kept fairly tidy to ensure good rotation of the pattern.

As with any new skill, you will need to practice and play around with your results.

My examples are first drafts with no pre-planning, as this is part of the fun in seeing where the patterns go.

I've used flora as my influence. However, feel free to use whatever shapes and influences you like.

When starting out, it's a good idea to use the images that you already like to draw.

Starting with the same steps as the previous example.

Step 1: Let your mind relax.

Step 2: Do the breathing exercise outlined on page xvii.

Step 3: Pick up your pen and notebook. In this example I am working with a 0.5 Unipin so it is easier to see the details.

Step 4: Choose a shape or line. In this example, I start with two wavy lines and a circle.

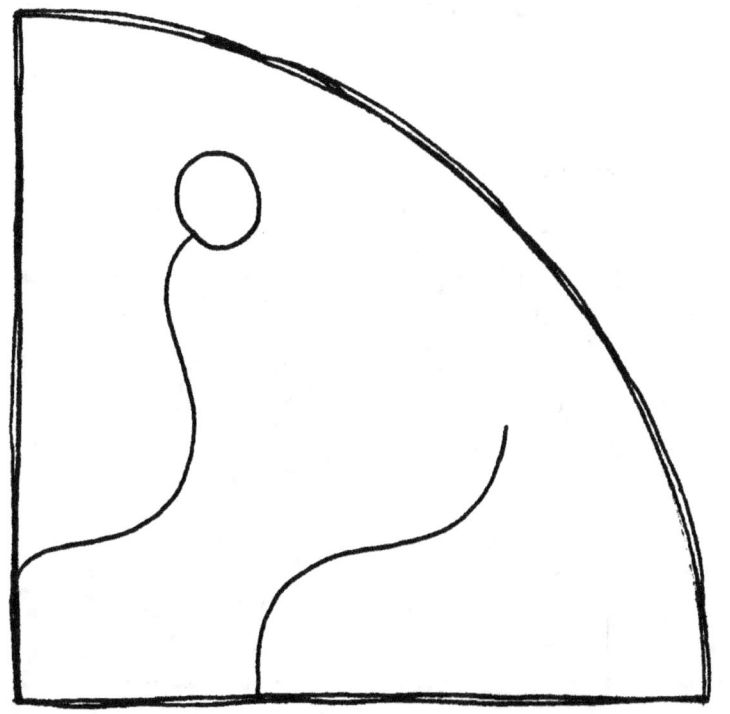

Step 5: Add more lines and details.

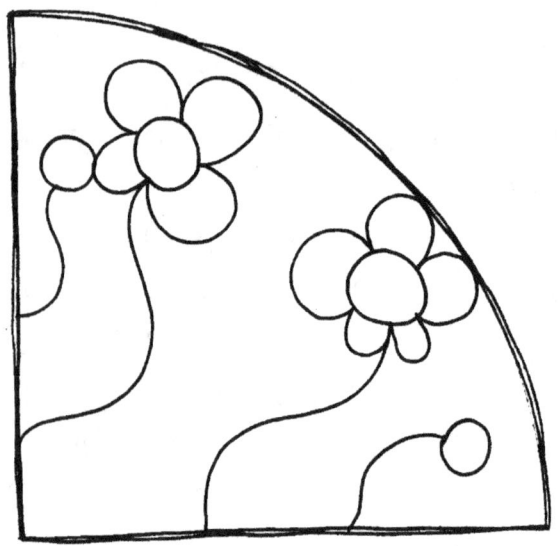

Step 6: Continue to add details.

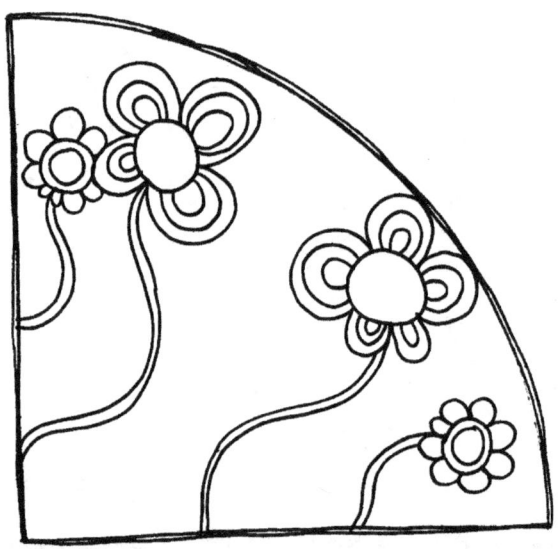

Step 7: Start to fill in space. Add in foliage.

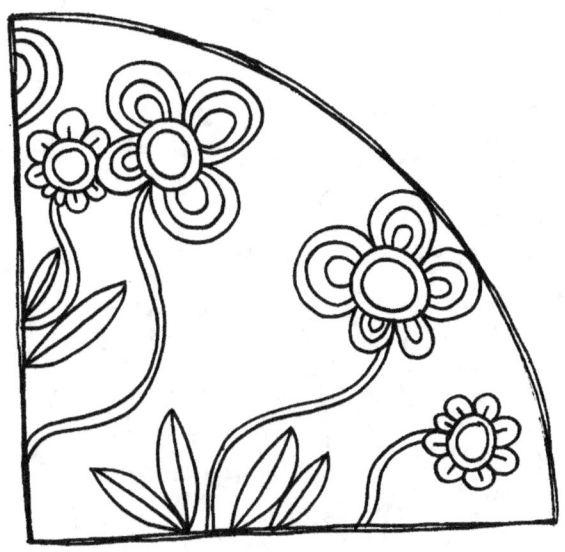

Step 8: More detail and more foliage.

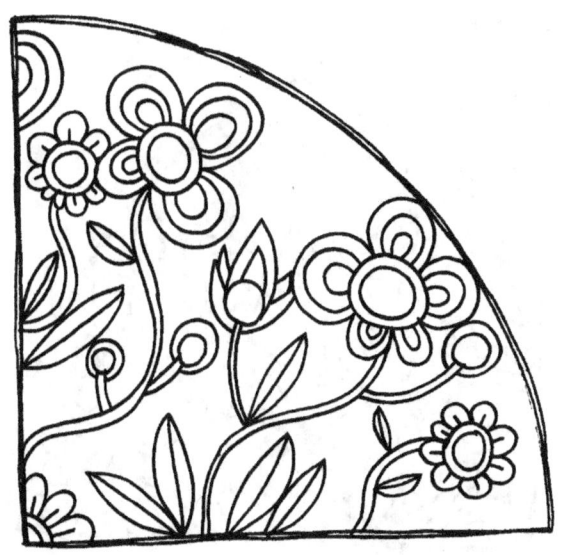

Step 9: Slowly add more detail until you are happy with your pattern.

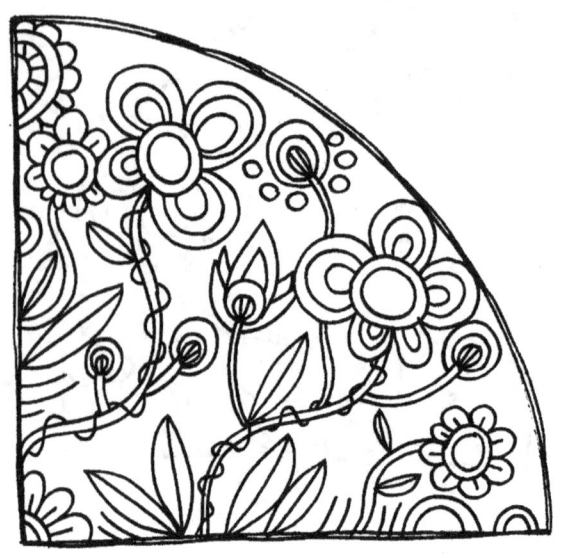

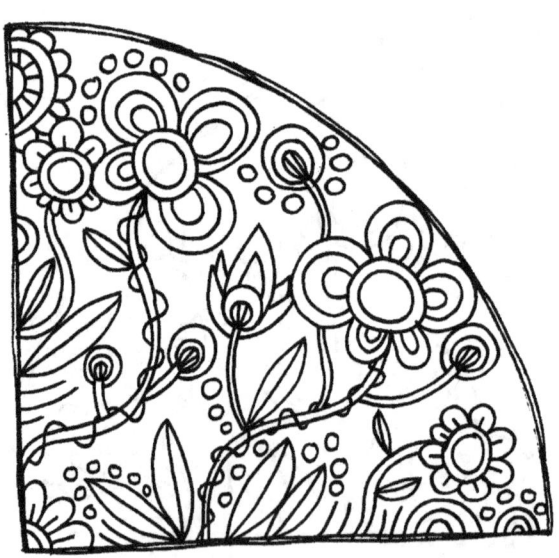

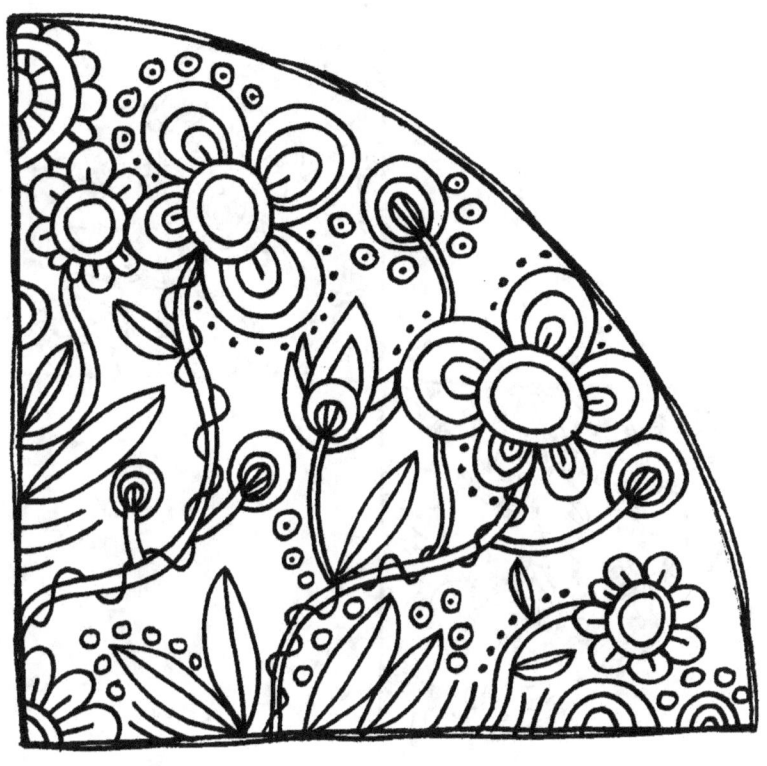

Now it's time to put it all together.

Duplicate the image to create the oppo-site piece of the image.

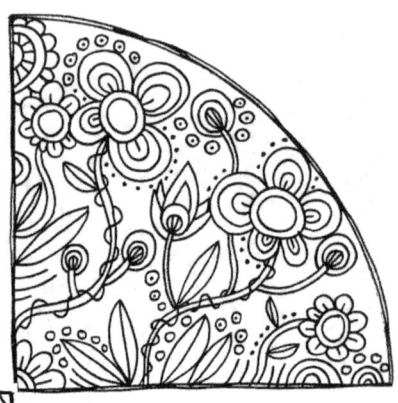

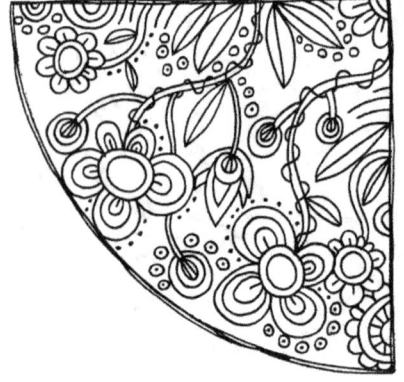

Next you will need to 'flip' your pattern in order to fit the final two pieces of the image.

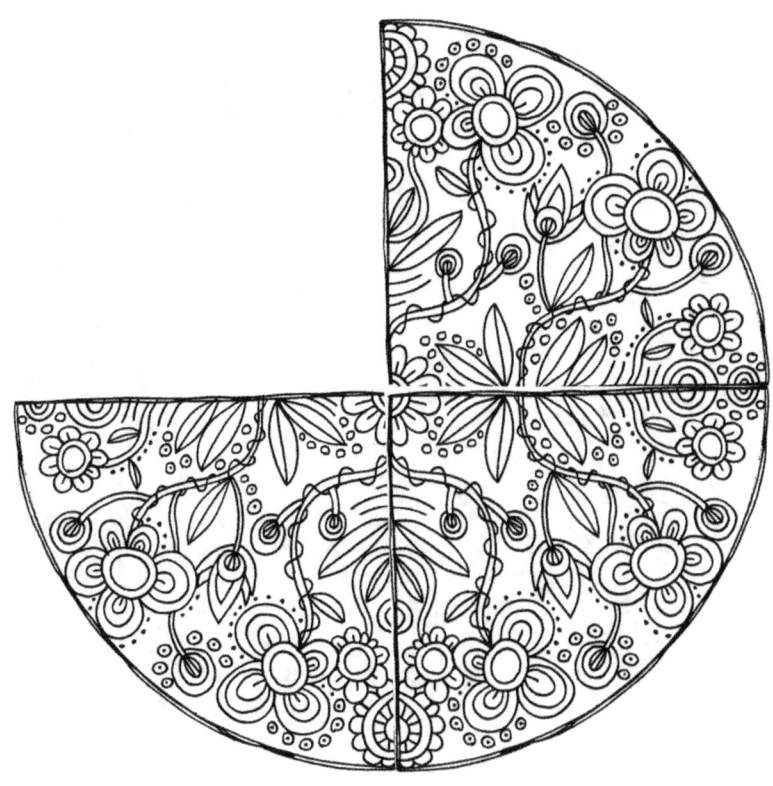

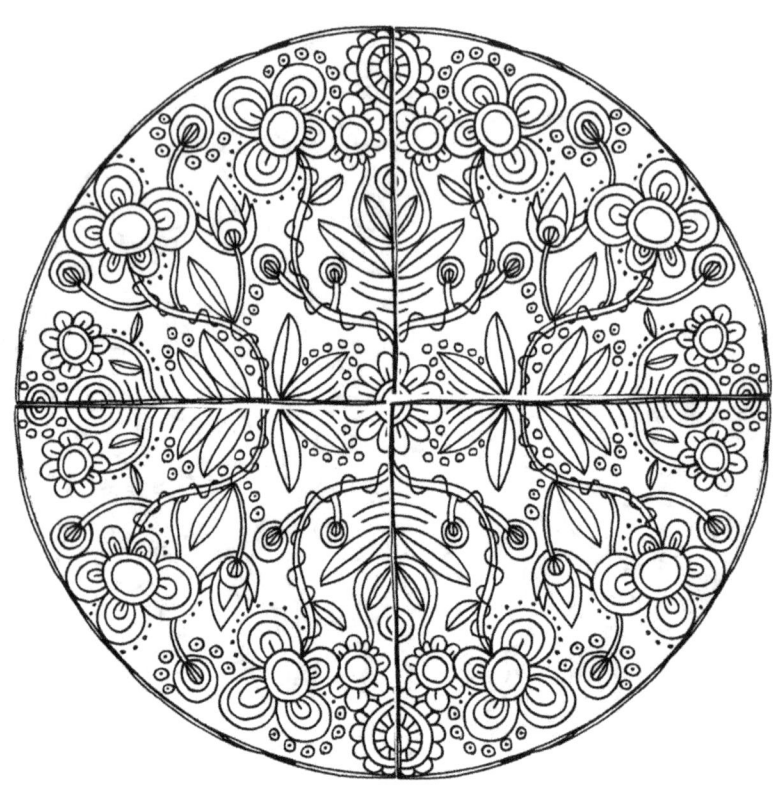

You can delete the join lines in a photo editing program, or you can use pencil for your template so the lines can be erased before you copy your image.

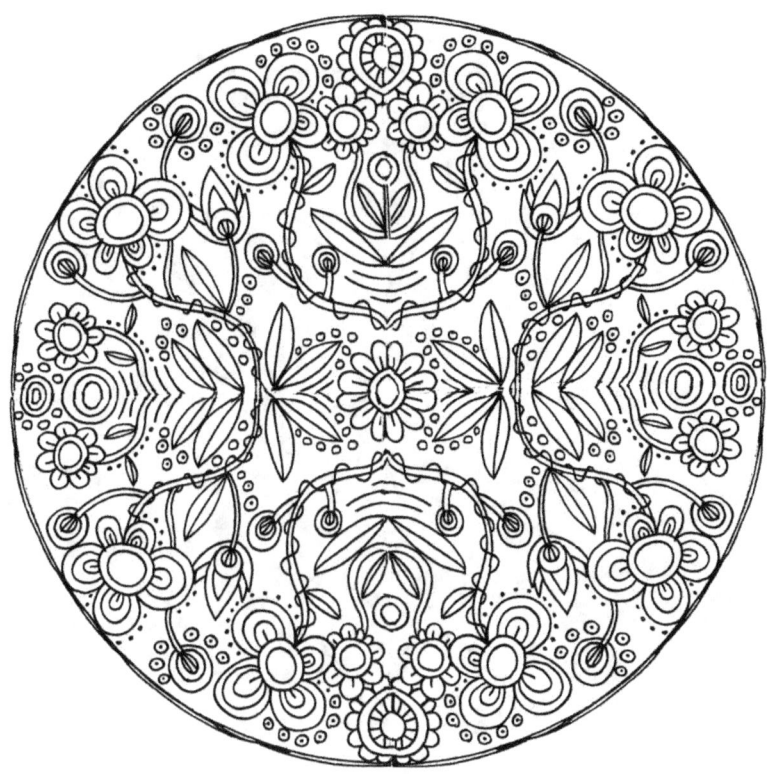

Practice Here

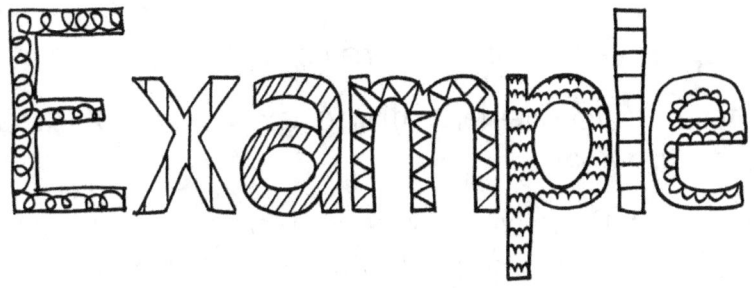

THREE

MARVELLOUS MACHINES

Drawing marvellous machines is loads of fun.

Let's see what you can create with these step-by-step images.

Remember those important first three steps...

Step 1: Let your mind relax.

Step 2: Do the breathing exercise outlined on page xvii.

Step 3: Pick up your pen and notebook. Again, I am working with a 0.5 Unipin.

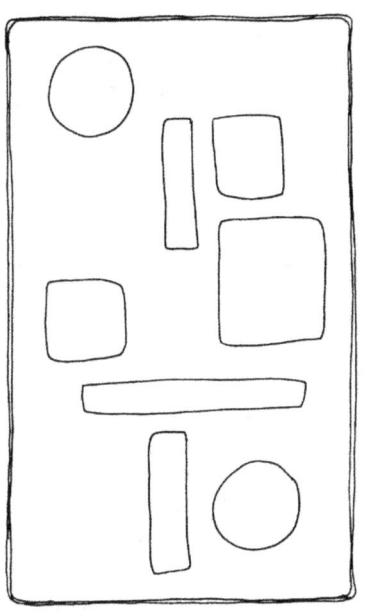

Step 4: Start with some basic shapes. I've used rectangles, squares and circles. However, you can choose whatever shapes you want for your machine.

Step 5: Build on these shapes. For example, link them with tubes or pipes, and add details such a buttons and dials.

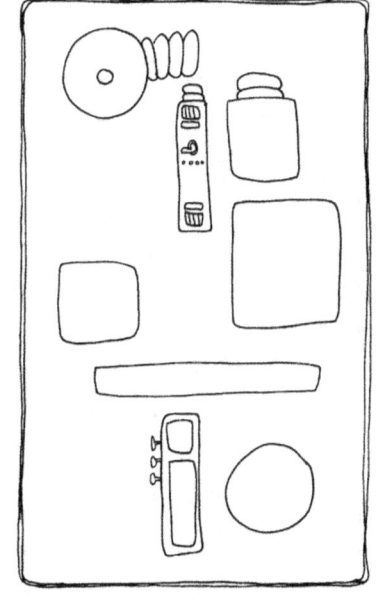

Step 6: Think about your machine. How will you turn it on? How will you control it? What will make this machine move?

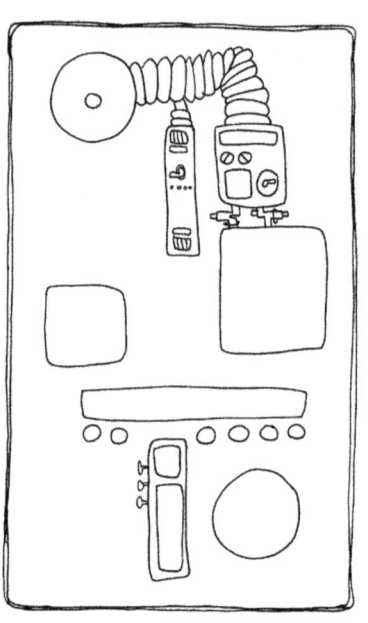

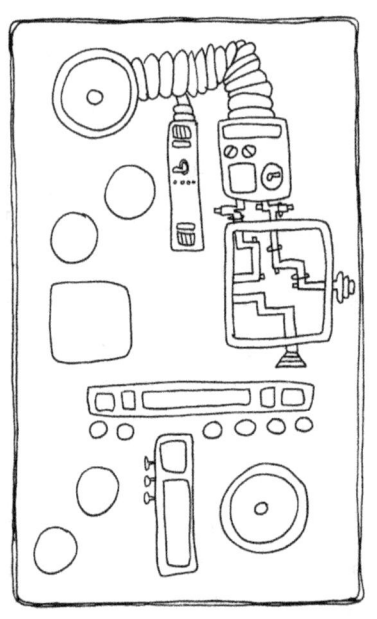

Step 7: Continue to add more details such as blinking lights, cords, cogs, wheels and movement.

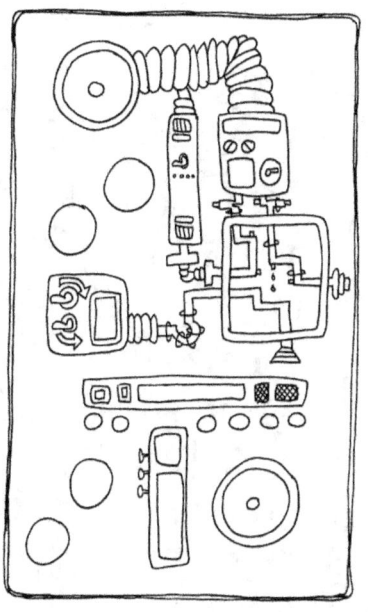
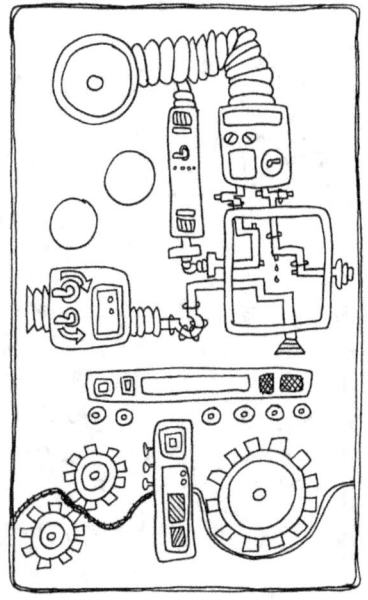
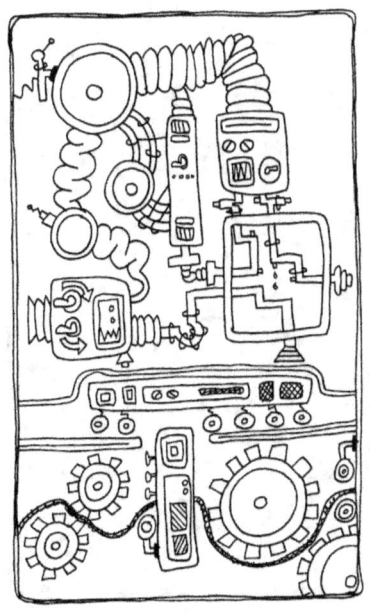
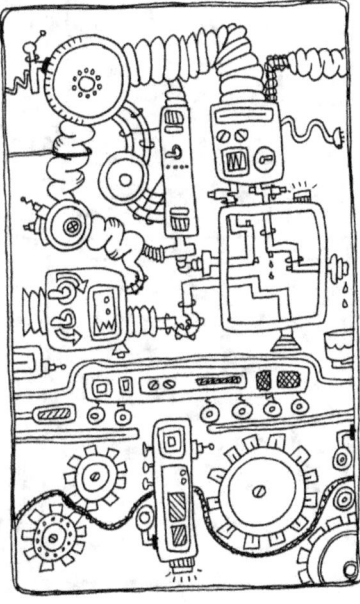

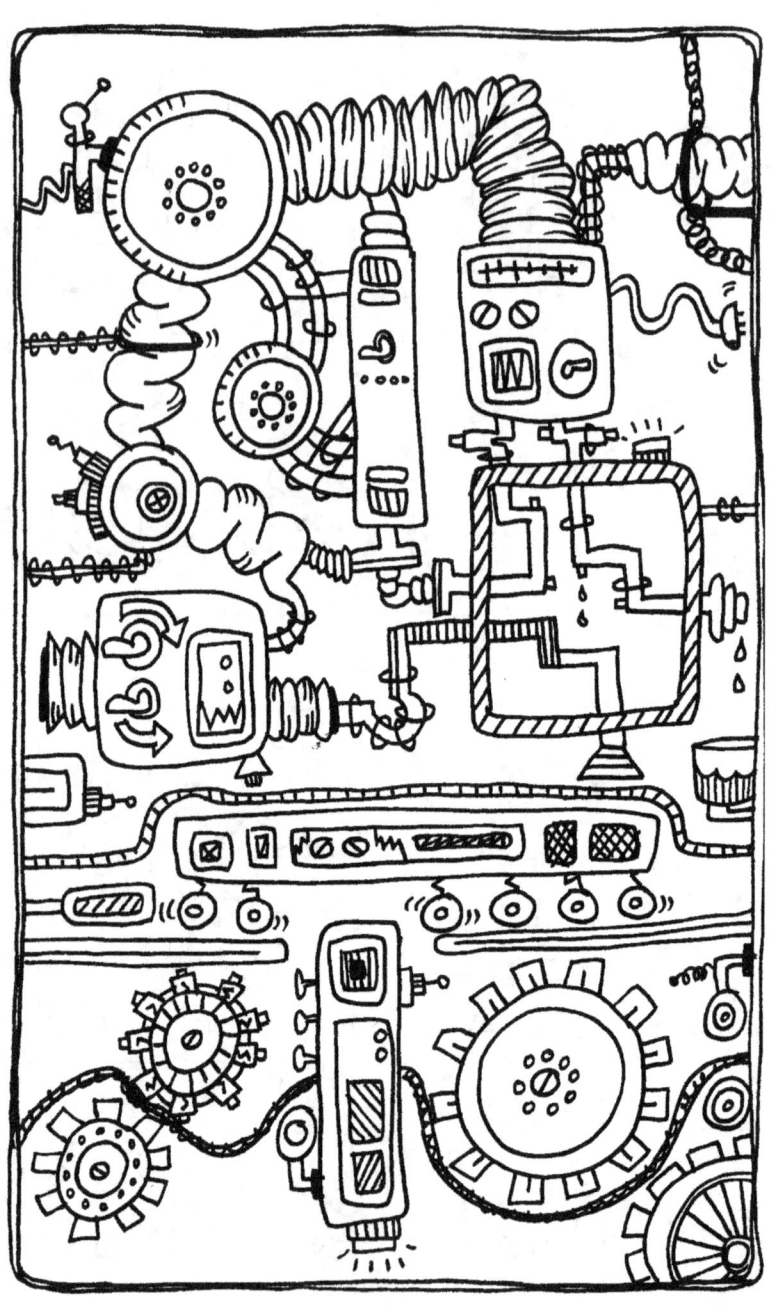

PART 2

Practice
Here

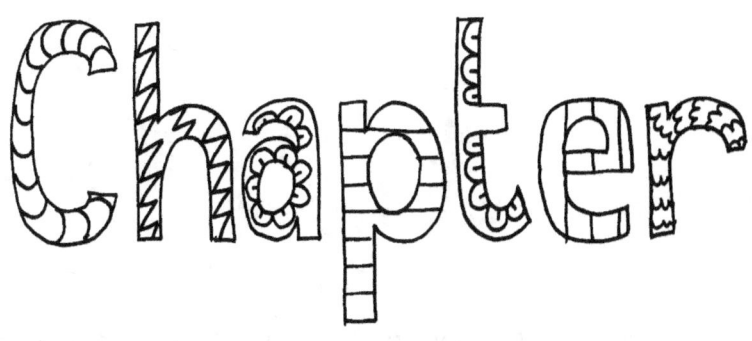

Chapter

ONE

LANDSCAPES

Over the years, I have been inspired by the landscapes around me, including natural and built environments.

I love to explore questions like 'how do humans and nature co-exist?' and 'what are the consequences of our choices when we build cities?'.

This chapter focuses on buildings and the skyline that they produce, but also includes natural lines that have been inspired by the plants around me at the time of the drawing.

I'm reminded of *Uno's Garden*, by Graeme Base, and the need to balance the concrete with nature in order to remain in harmony.

Brisbane

The sun was setting behind the city while I was sitting in the shade of a Jacaranda tree.

The light was shimmering and the breeze was cooling, while the waves of the river gently dispersed in crisscross patterns before me.

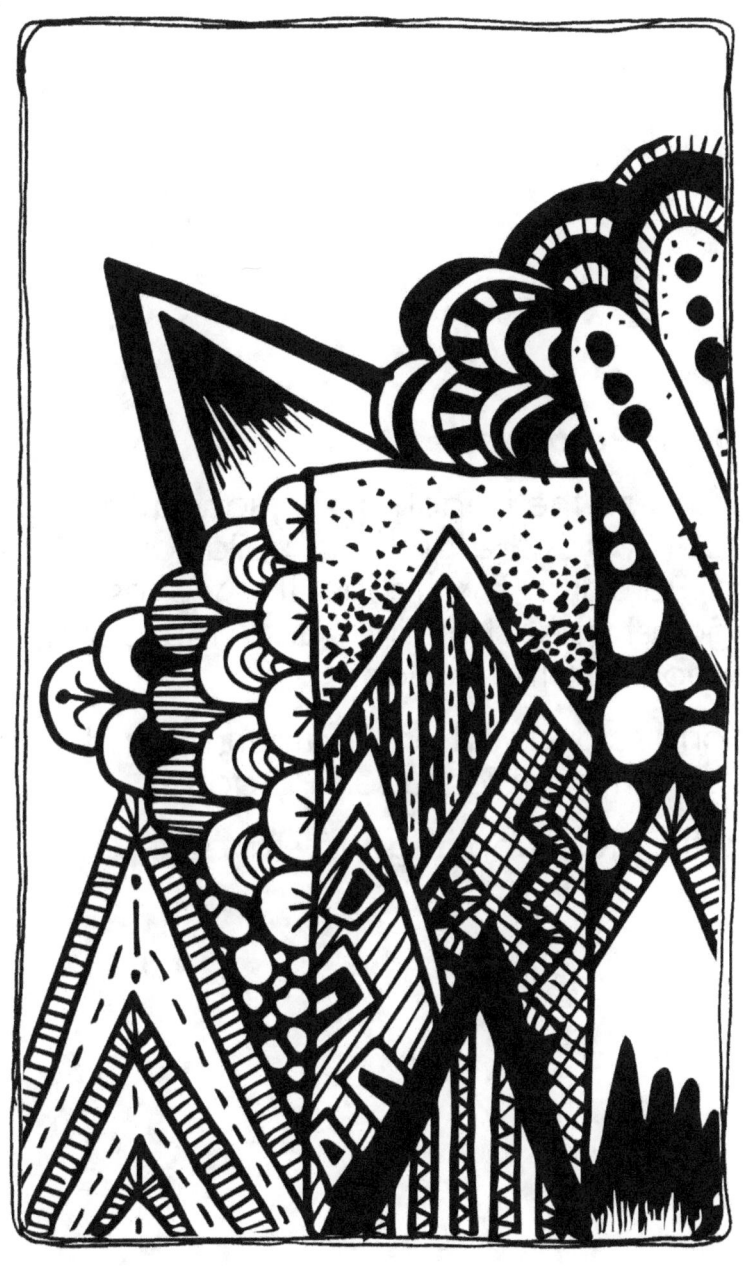

Surfers Paradise

Sitting on the beach at Coolangatta, look-ing towards the gigantic buildings of Surf-ers Paradise, I watched the waves crash against the shoreline and the seagulls swoop into the ocean.

Storm clouds where gathering and rain was imminent for Surfers Paradise.

Fortunately Coolangatta stayed dry.

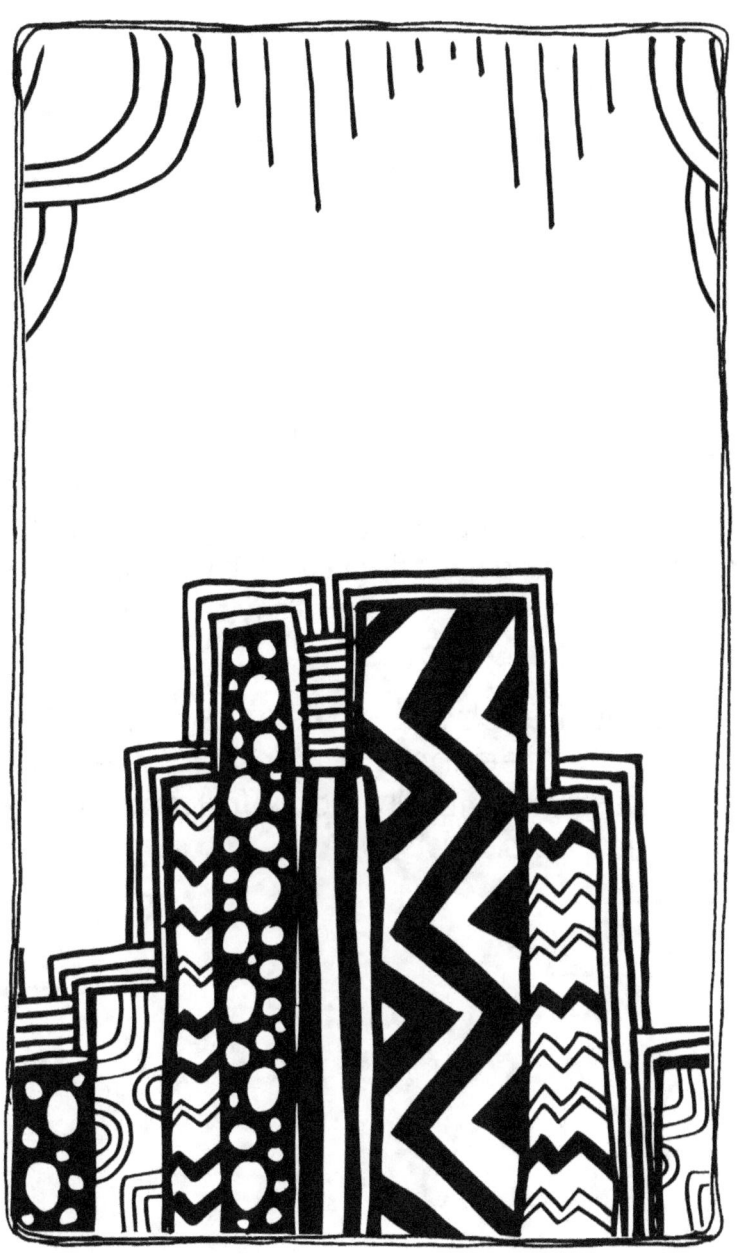

Hinterland

On a weekend away in the Noosa Valley, I found myself reflecting on a beautiful view of the Maroochy River with Mount Ninderry in the background.

I was inspired by the clear sky, the cool wind, the greenness all around me, and the lake filled with lily pads (reminding me of the Impressionists).

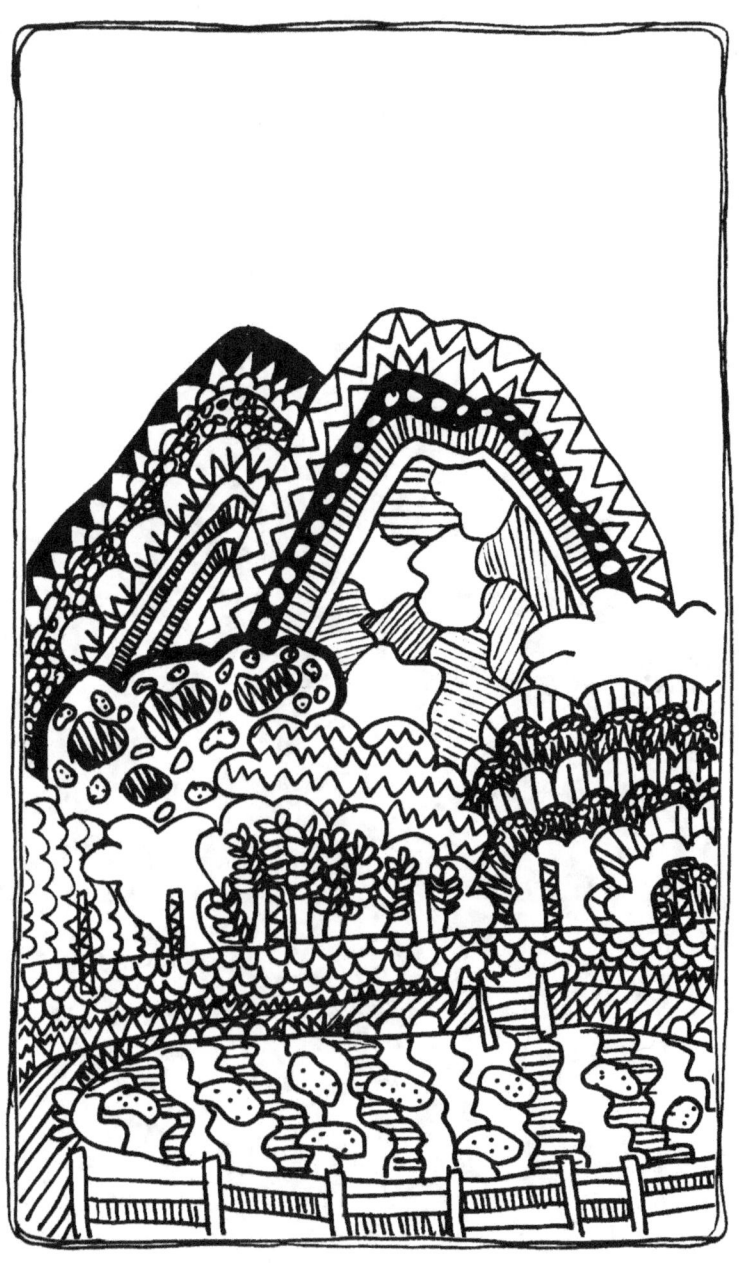

Your cityscape

Your countryscape

Your _____ scape

NOTES:

NOTES:

Practice Here

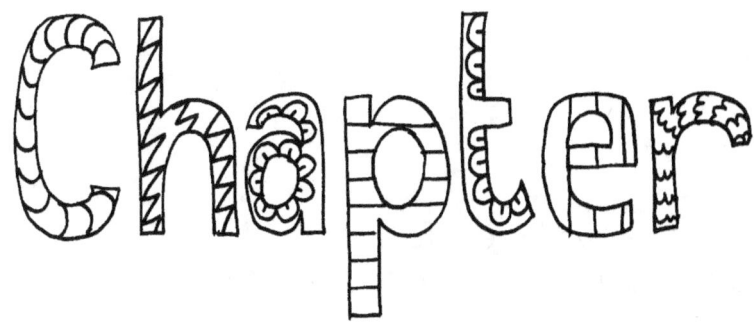

TWO

FLORA

I've always been fascinated by the structure of plants and their tenacity for survival.

The way they emerge from a seed, the way they coexist in small spaces, and the way they continue to adapt to their environments.

The mathematician in me, is also fascinated by the plant kingdom's application of the golden section rule, also known as Phi, the golden mean, or the golden ratio.

If you're interested in learning more, Bloomsbury's *The Golden Section: Nature's Greatest Secret*, covers the maths and science, and its appearance in the natural and human worlds.

Tulips

Having received a tulip after the birth of one of my children, this flower has remained one of my favourites.

In this image, I was inspired by the distinct shape of the tulip, while reflecting on the joy and wonder of children, and the challenges of caring for a newborn baby.

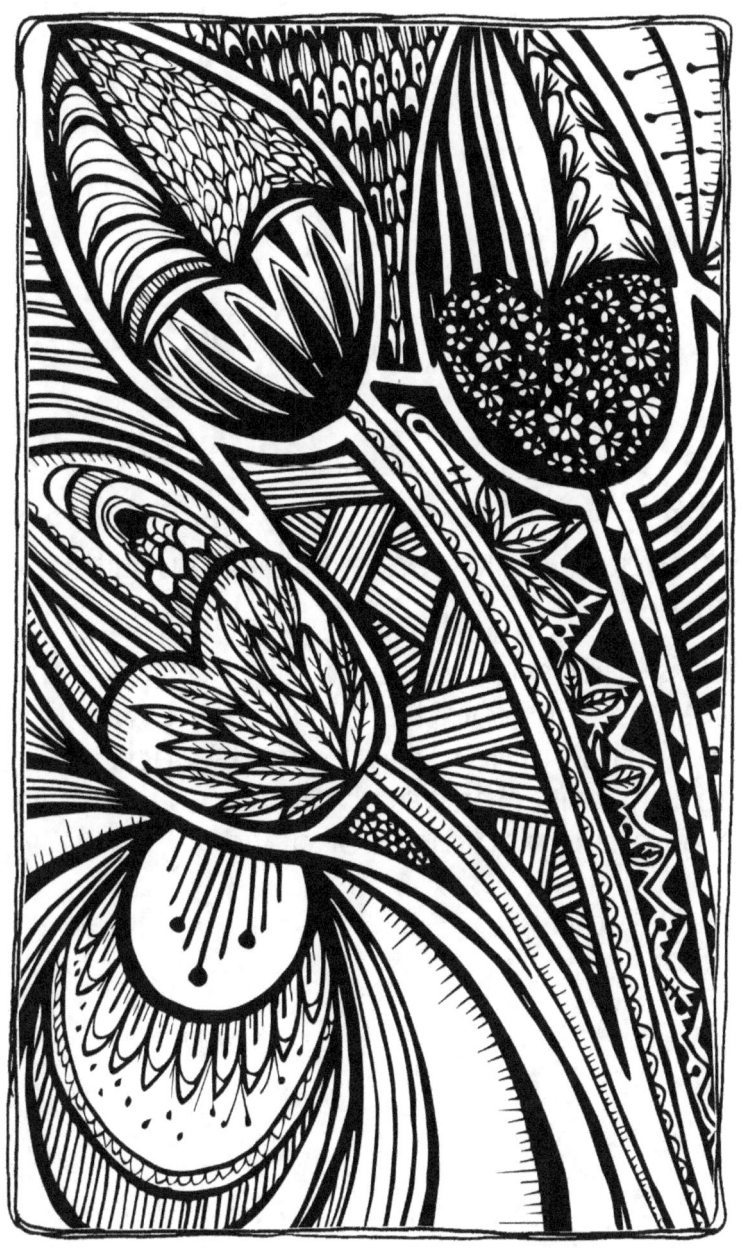

Bouquet

A bouquet of flowers is a beautiful gift from nature.

In this image I tried something a little different: I drew images from various viewpoints – like Picasso in his cubist period – and carried the different perspectives across the page to give a multidimensional view.

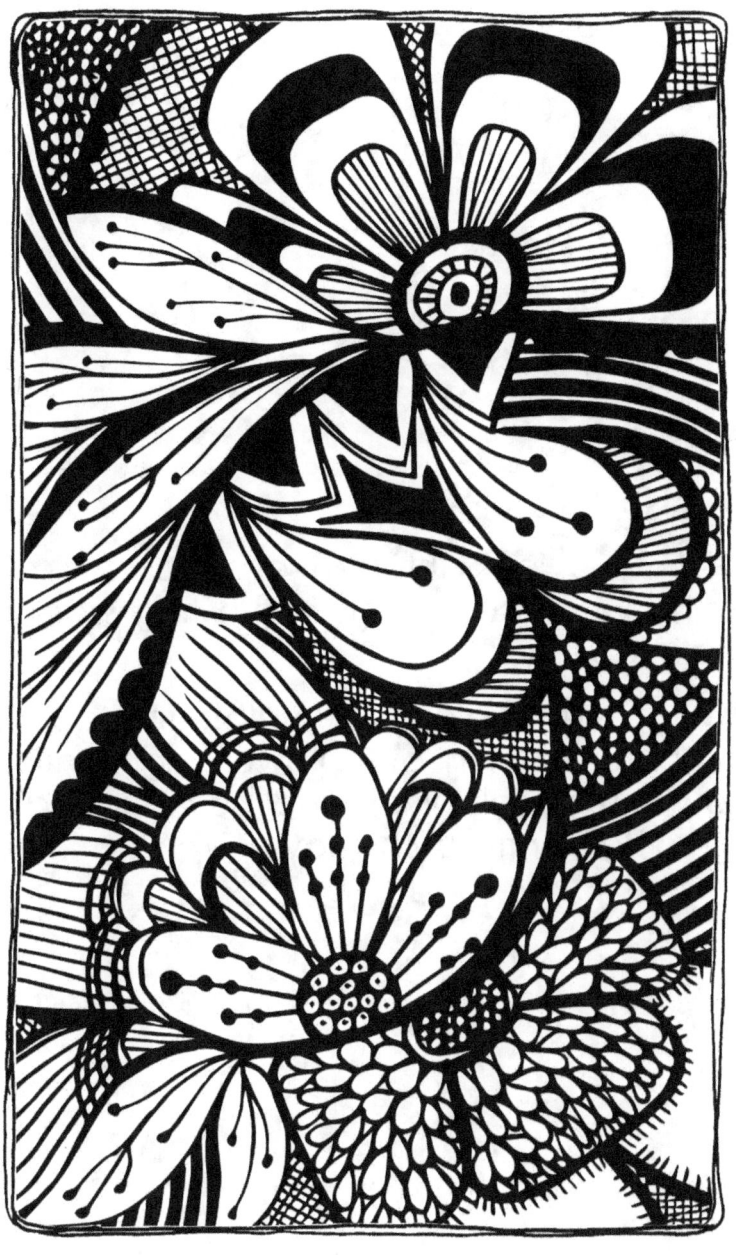

Petals

When we look through a specific viewpoint, we focus on an interesting slice of the image.

Here I've used a circle template to magnify a particular part of a flower, highlighting how the petals, lines and curves radiate from the centre of the flower.

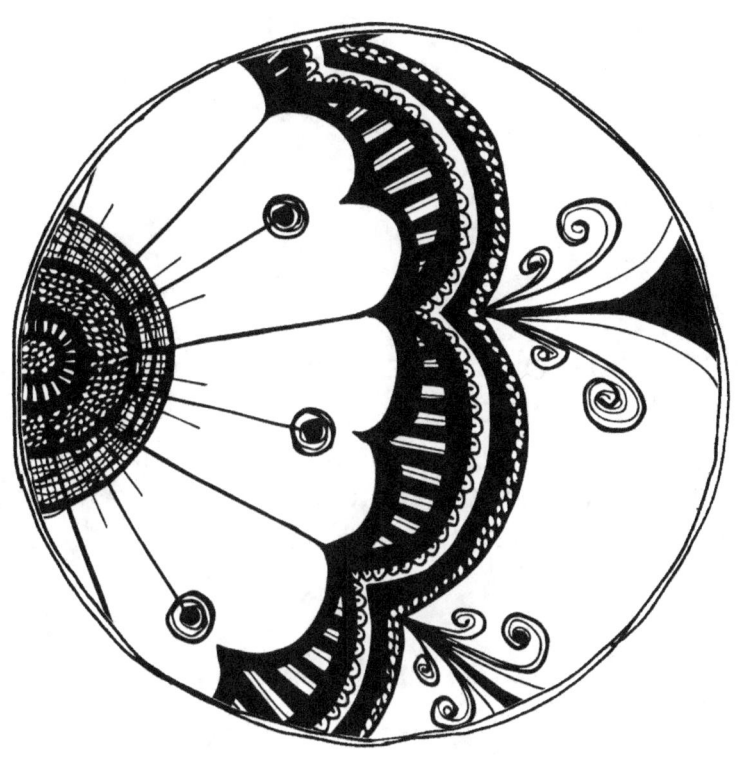

Buds

This image also uses a circle template as a guide to produce a pattern. I've continued with the tulip theme, combining parts of the plant's leaf pattern with curved lines as visual links.

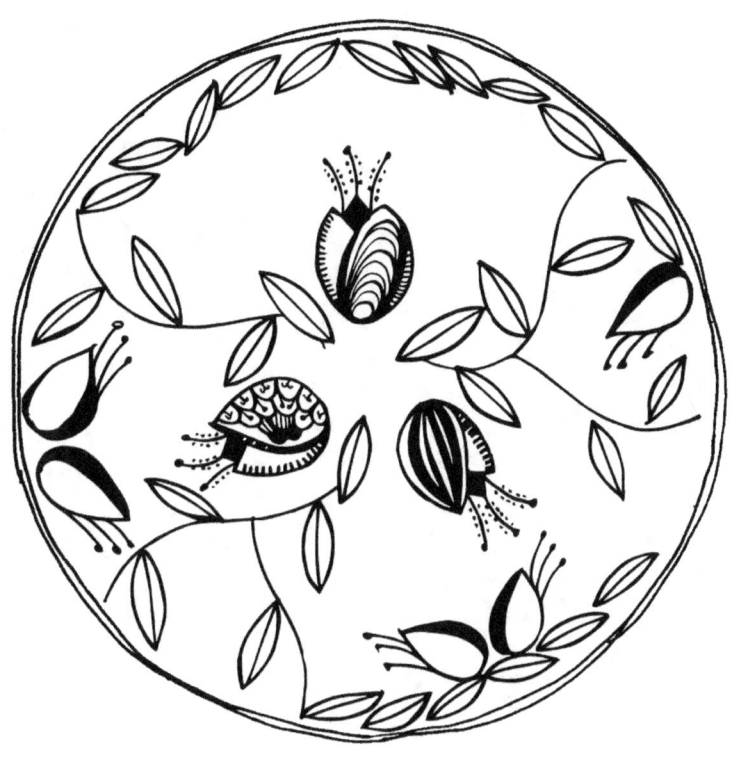

Your flower

Your bouquet

Your petals

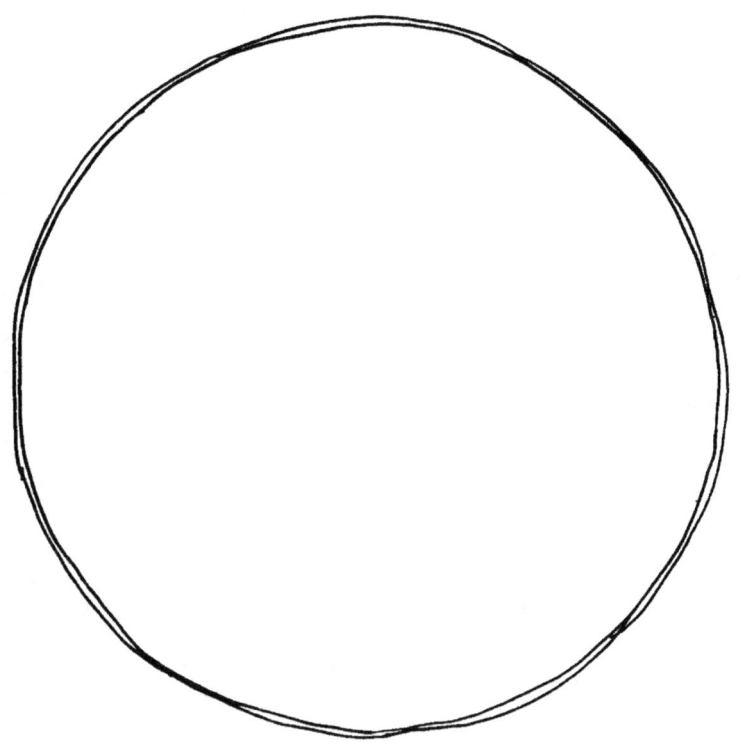

Your buds

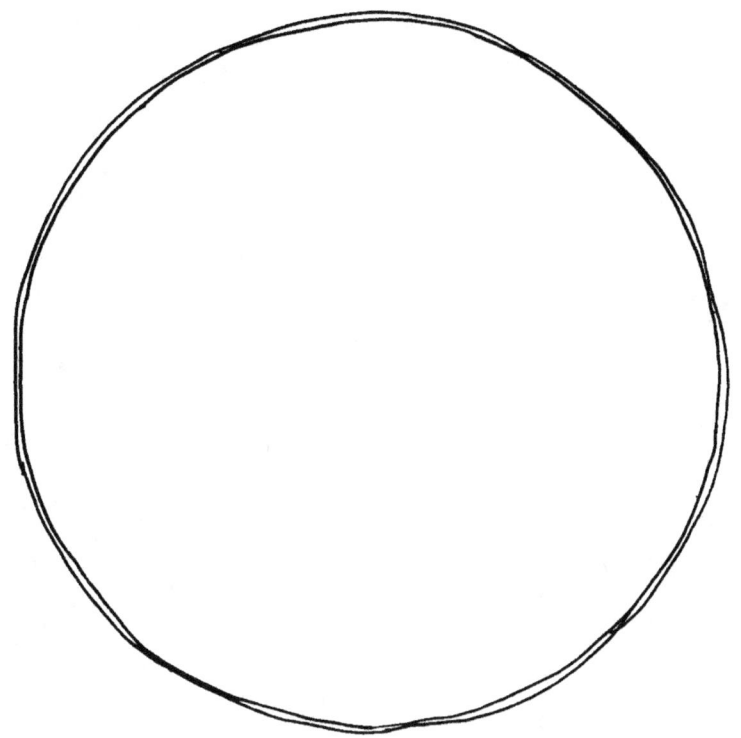

NOTES:

NOTES:

Practice
Here
↙

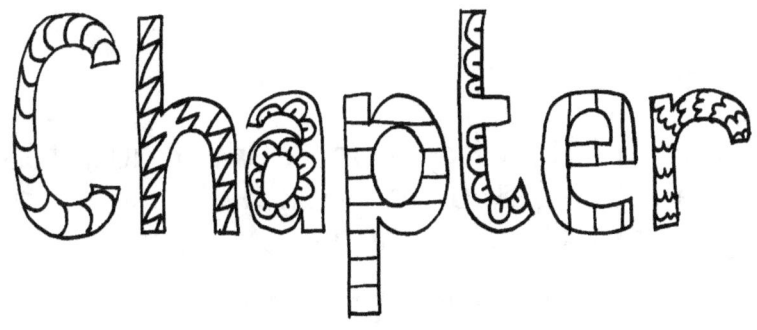

THREE

REPEATING PATTERNS

My sister-in-law gave one of my daughters a beautiful colouring book by the international bestseller, Joanna Basford.

Intrigued by the images, I read up on Joanna's work and learned that she likes to repeat her images by flipping and rotating them in Photoshop.

I couldn't resist trying the technique in my own tangles.

It's a clever way to create perfectly symmetrical images, especially if – like most of us – you struggle with freehand symmetry.

While some people think it's cheating to use a computer, I believe that the talent lies in the drawing of the original image. So why not use the technological tools we have available?

Quarter circle

The idea is to create a simple effective pattern that can be repeated.

Make sure that your original template is as neat as possible; this will make it easier to repeat the pattern and fit it together to make the full circle.

Remember that creating the final circle is not just a matter of copying the quarter and fitting four of them together; you will need to flip two of the quarters in order for the sides to join up symmetrically (As demonstrated in the *Repeat Pattern Example*, page 17).

If you're not familiar with photo editing software like Photoshop, you can scan the image in black and white. Once you have the scanned image on your computer screen you will be able to 'flip' it using the menu item tools.

You will need to print two copies of the original version and two copies of the 'flipped' version. Cut them out and then stick together to create a full circle.

Copy the constructed image to allow you to create the final image.

Quarter circle

This was one of the first designs that I did after watching a video by Joanna where she outlined her technique.

The lovely twisty vines and brooding flowers of her images inspired this design, and I particularly like the contrasting effect created by the delicate dots.

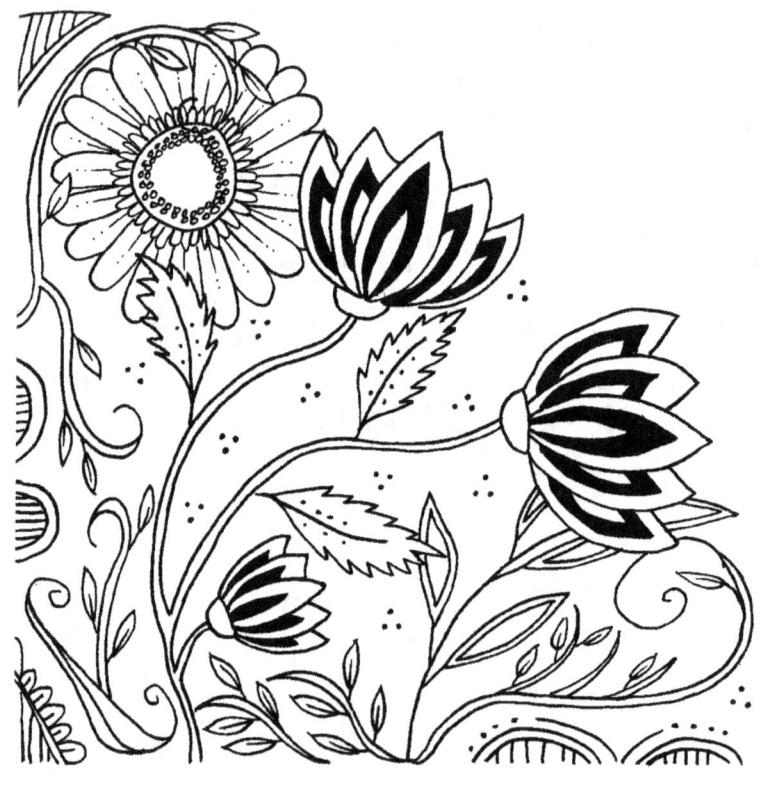

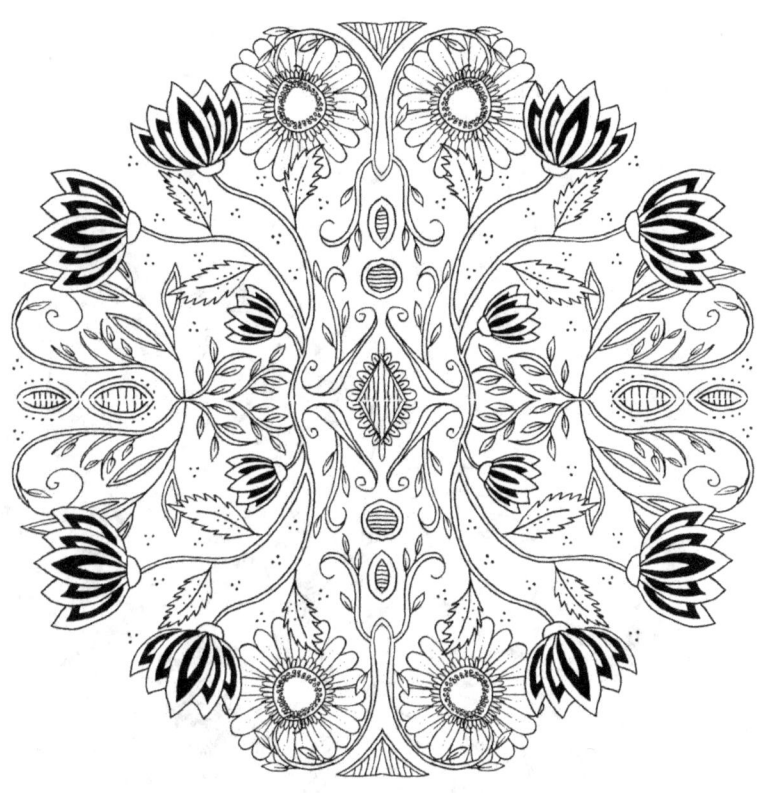

Quarter circle

What is a garden without butterflies?

This pattern was inspired by a walk in the park, where numerous butterflies kept flying around us.

What is your favourite insect when walking in the garden or park?

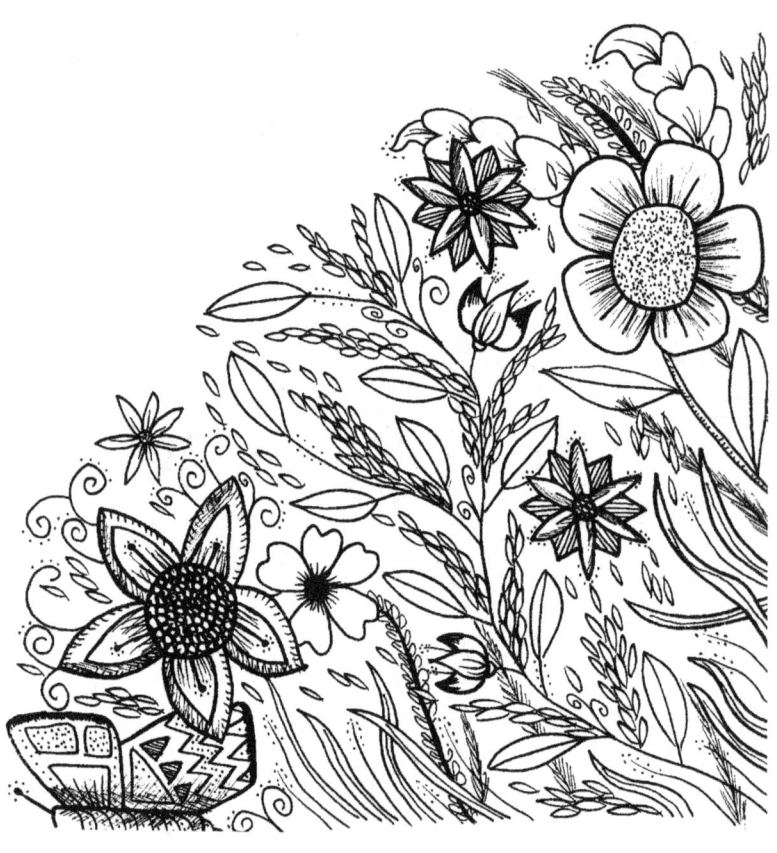

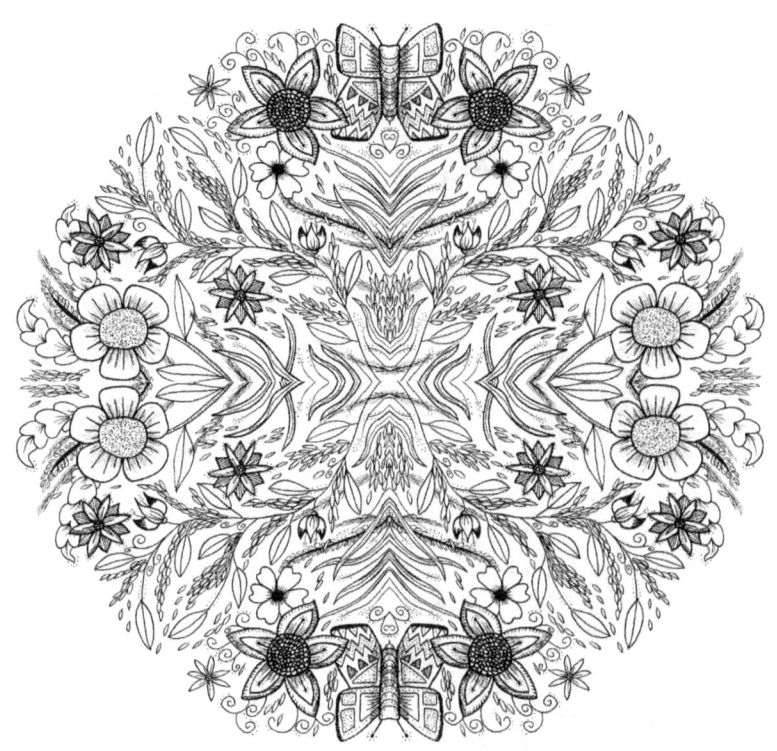

Quarter diamond

While circles are nice, some people may prefer the sharper lines of a diamond.

The lines in this image were inspired by the pavers, pebbles and wooden features of a Zen garden.

Use the same process for repeating the shape to create the whole, as we did for the quarter circle.

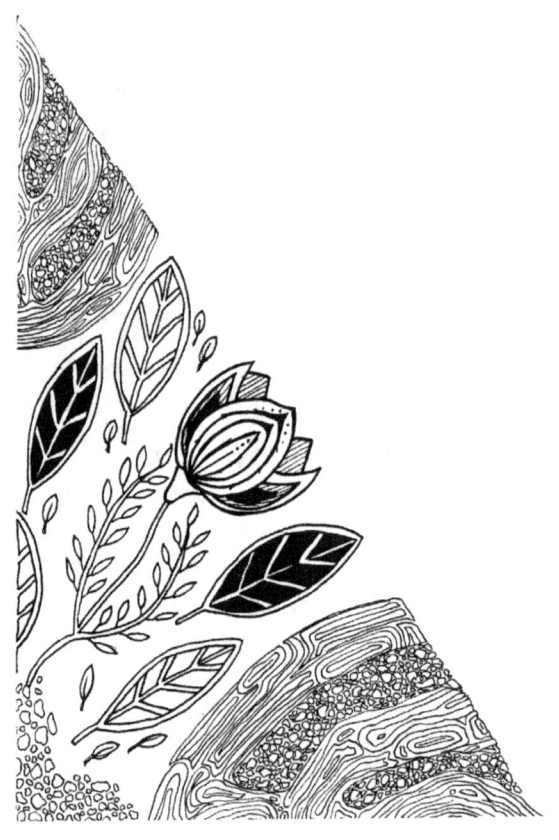

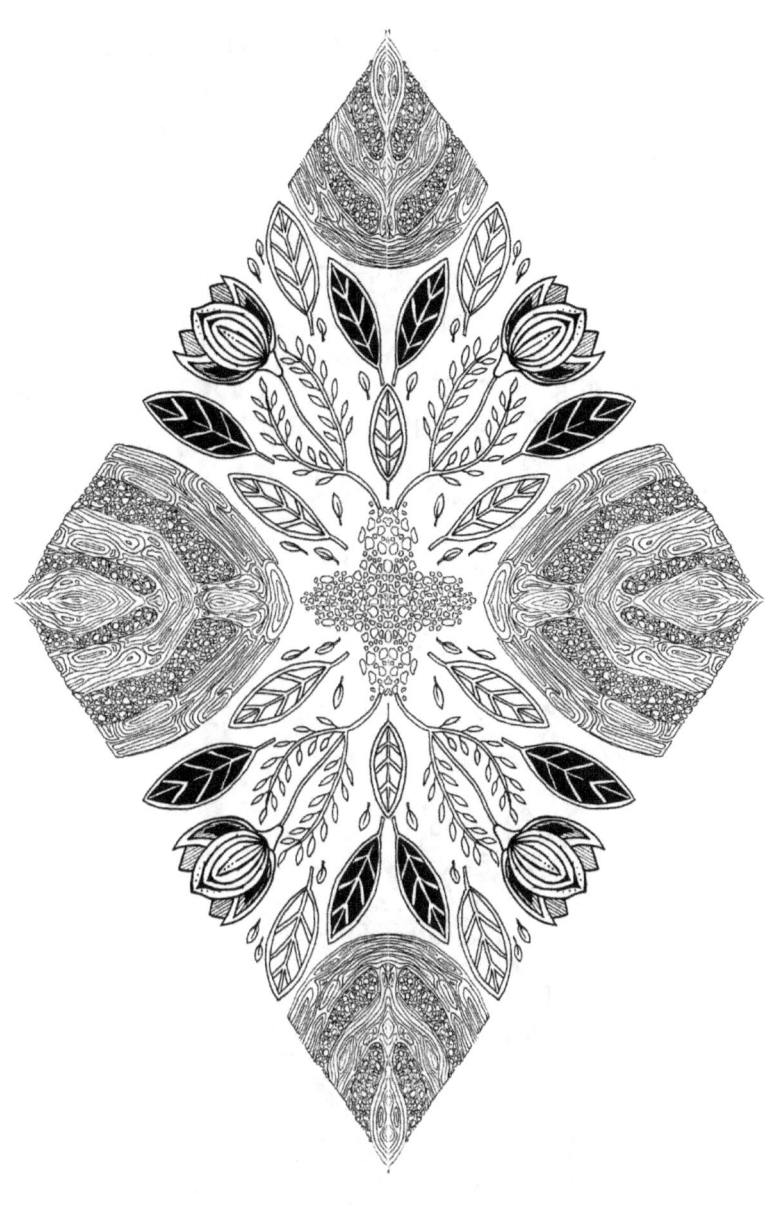

Quarter diamond

Try creating a marvellous machine with this template. What weird and wonderful apparatus might you need to make your machine work?

I like tubes that look like your insides! How about some crazy aerials? Who knows what signals these machines rely on to operate.

The kids said it must make diamonds, because it is shaped like one.

What do you think?

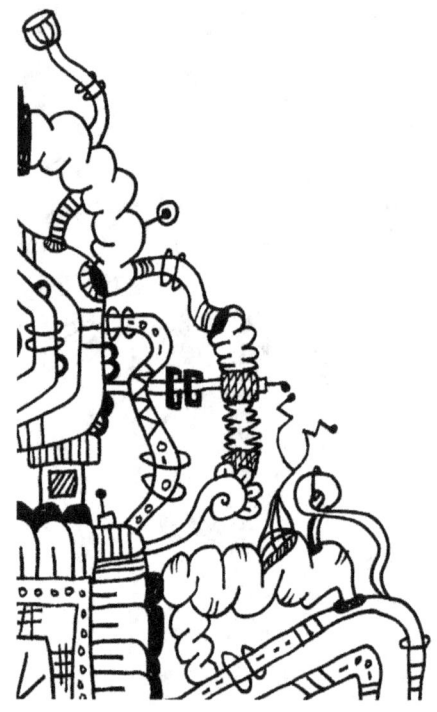

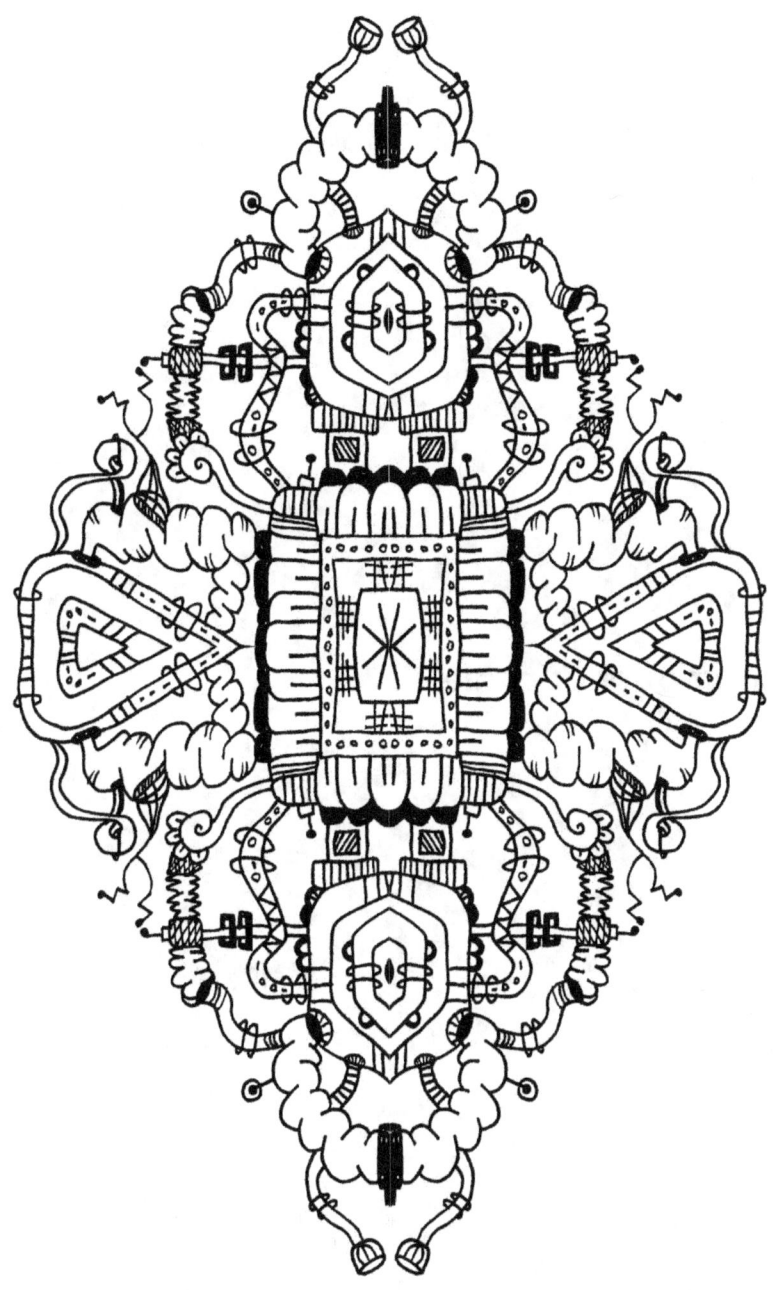

Your quarter circle

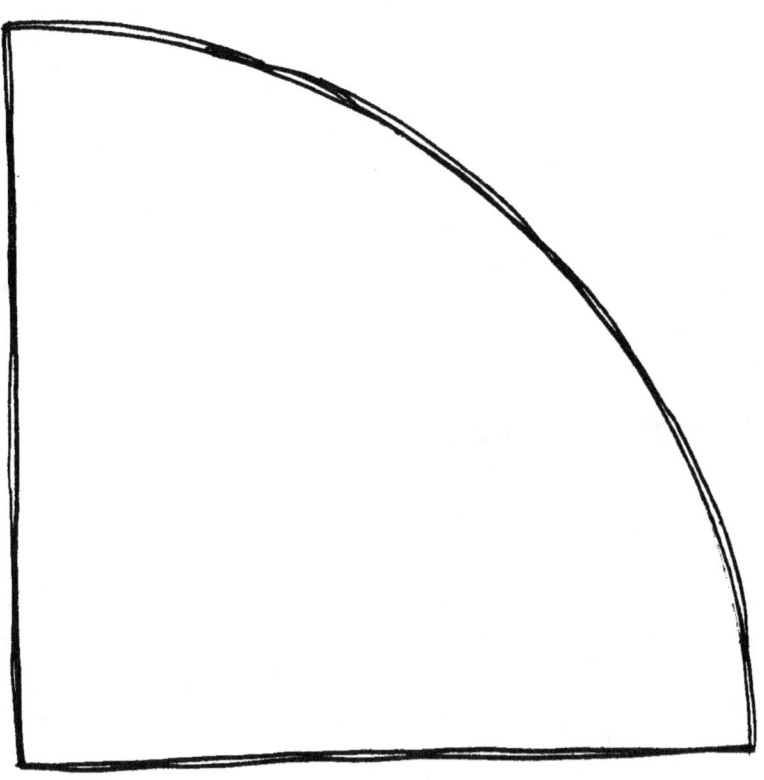

Your quarter circle

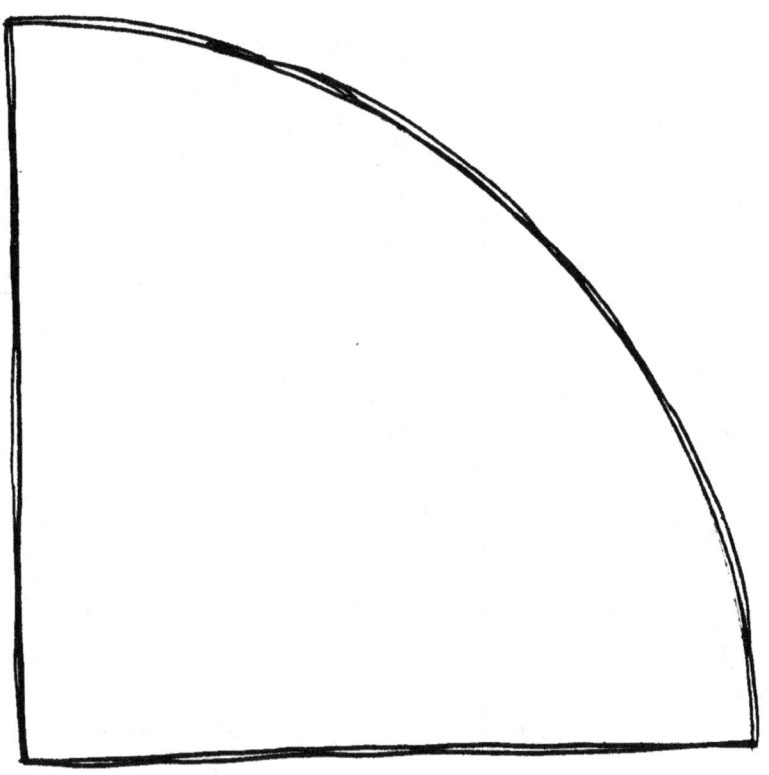

Your quarter diamond

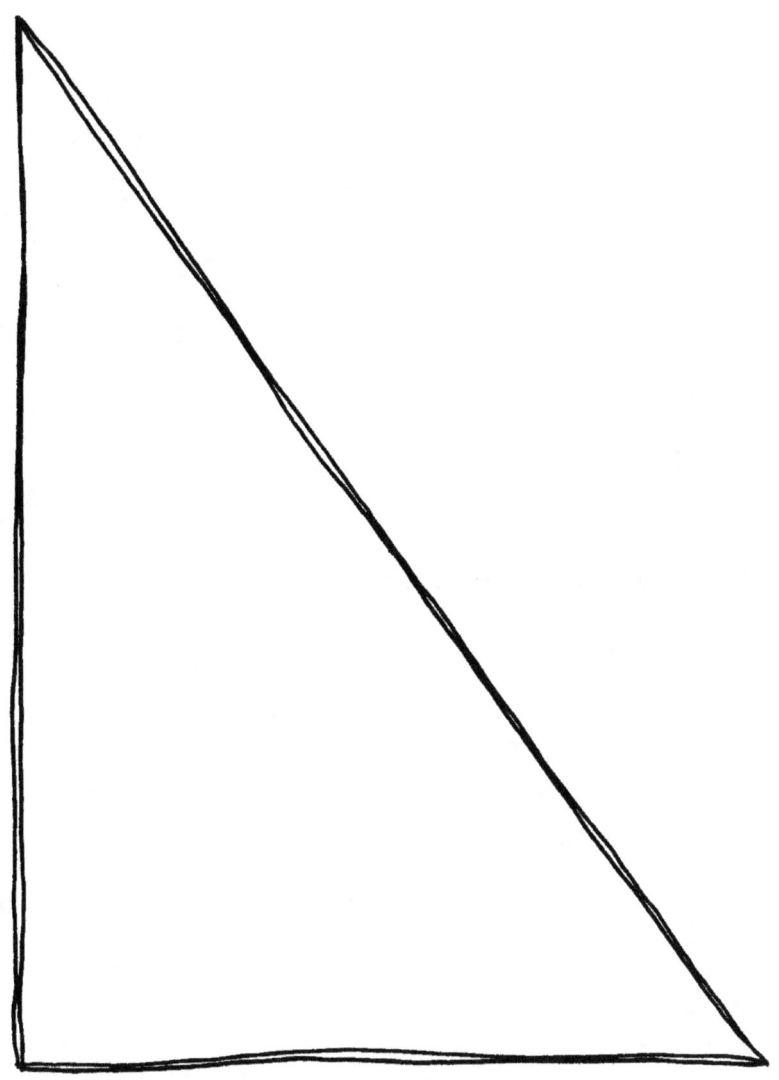

Your quarter diamond

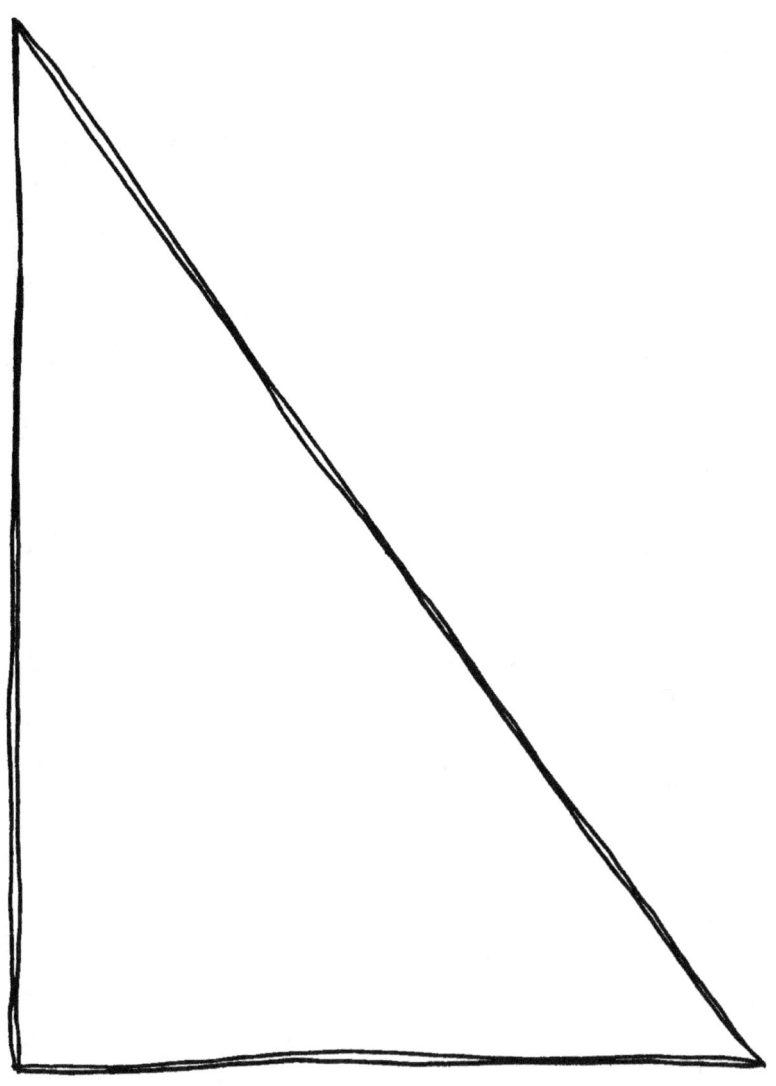

NOTES:

NOTES:

Practice
Here

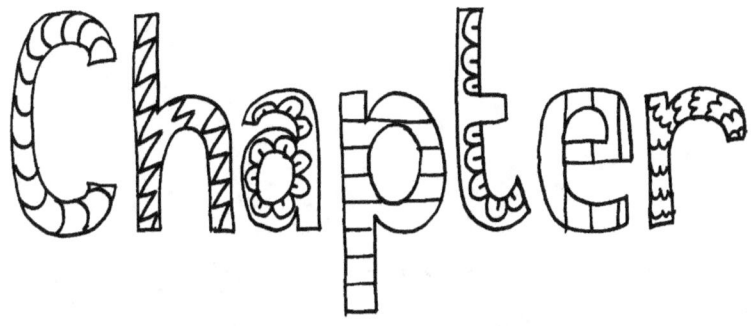

FOUR

LOVELY LETTERS

The shape of a letter is a great starting point for a design, and will often come with special significance because of a name or word.

I've created the following letter designs inspired by people I know and their traits and personalities.

Letter G

It seems that children grow, grow, grow. Here the letter G can be seen to be growing in a tangled weave in all directions.

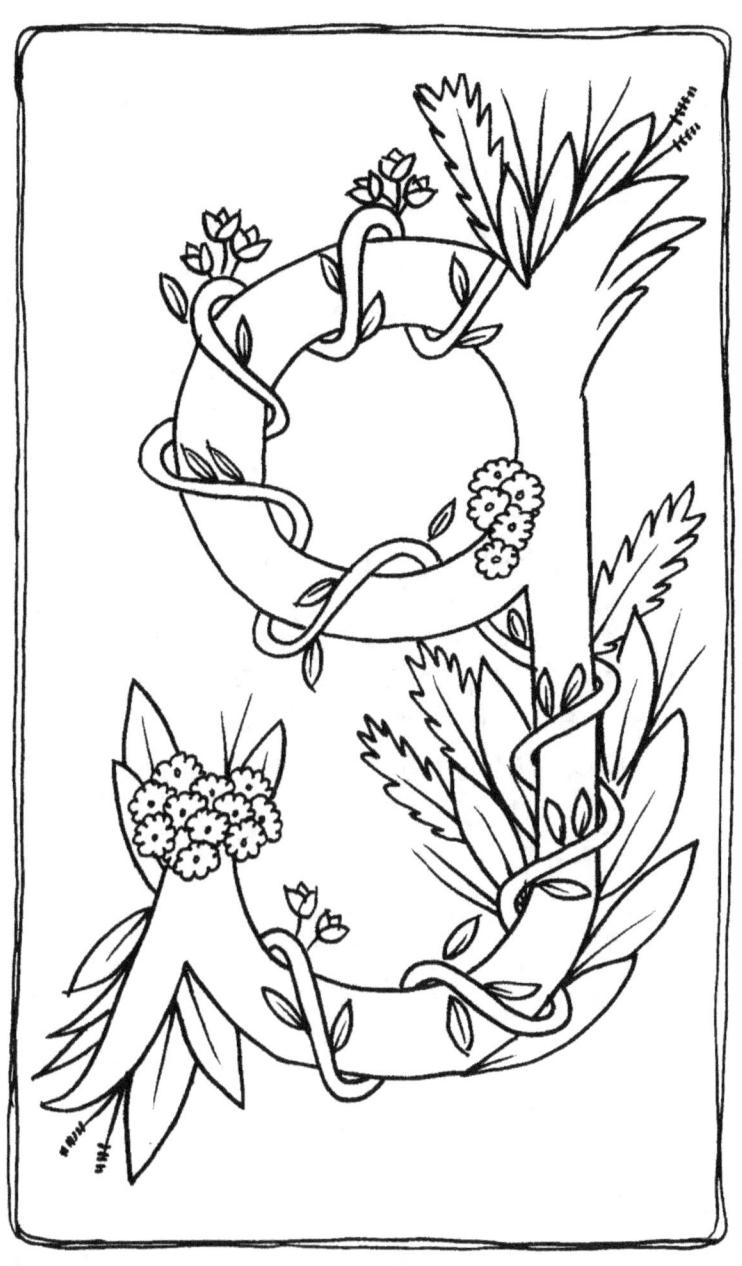

Letter S

This letter S is inspired by a person who embraces the world around them and revels in the beauty of nature.

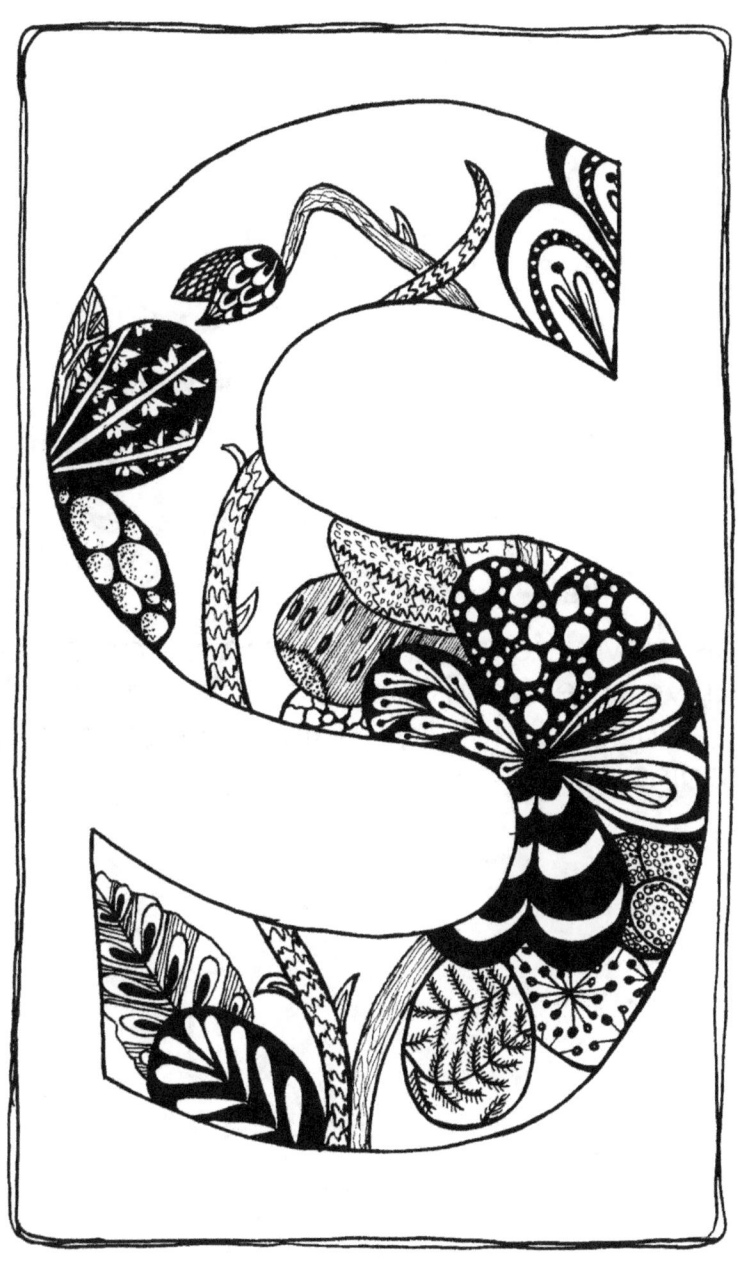

Letter S digital

This very different S is inspired by an alternative side of this person, drawn to analysis and technology – think Minecraft and coding.

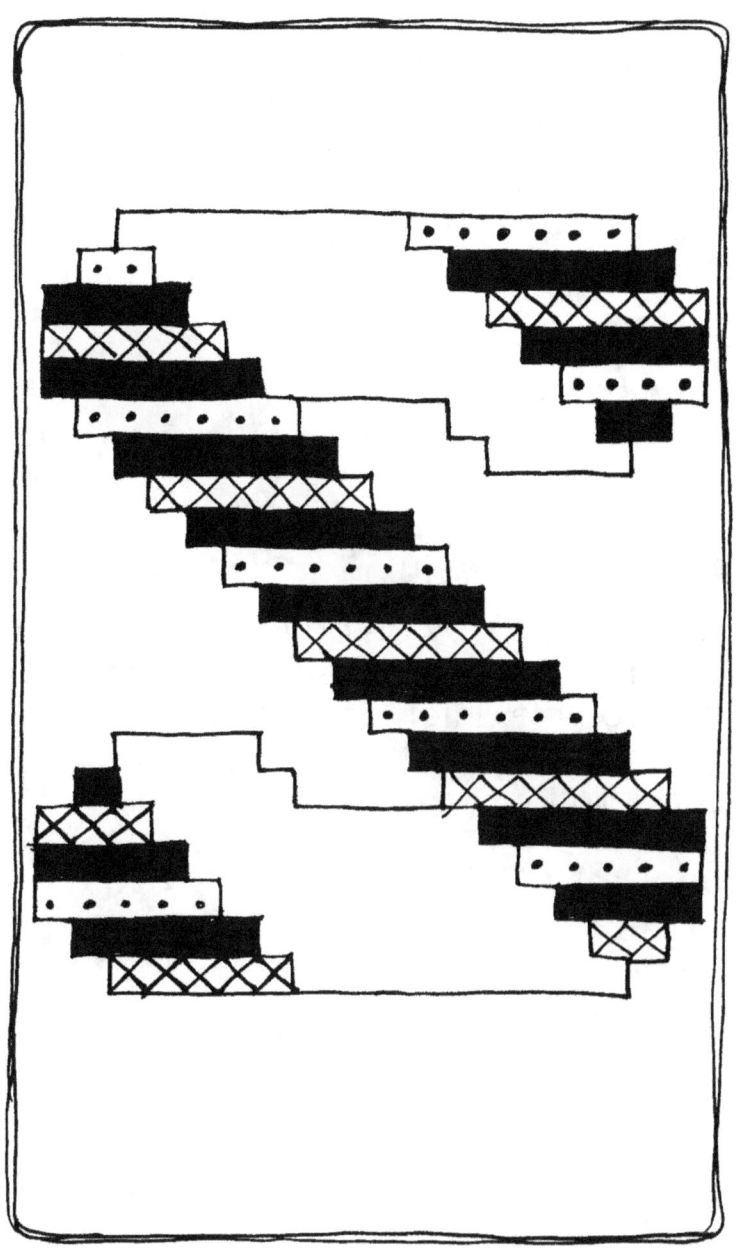

Letter L

This L is inspired by an action-packed, free spirit. Their dynamic personality is reflected in the complex intermingling of straight and curved lines, as well as the black and white optical illusions.

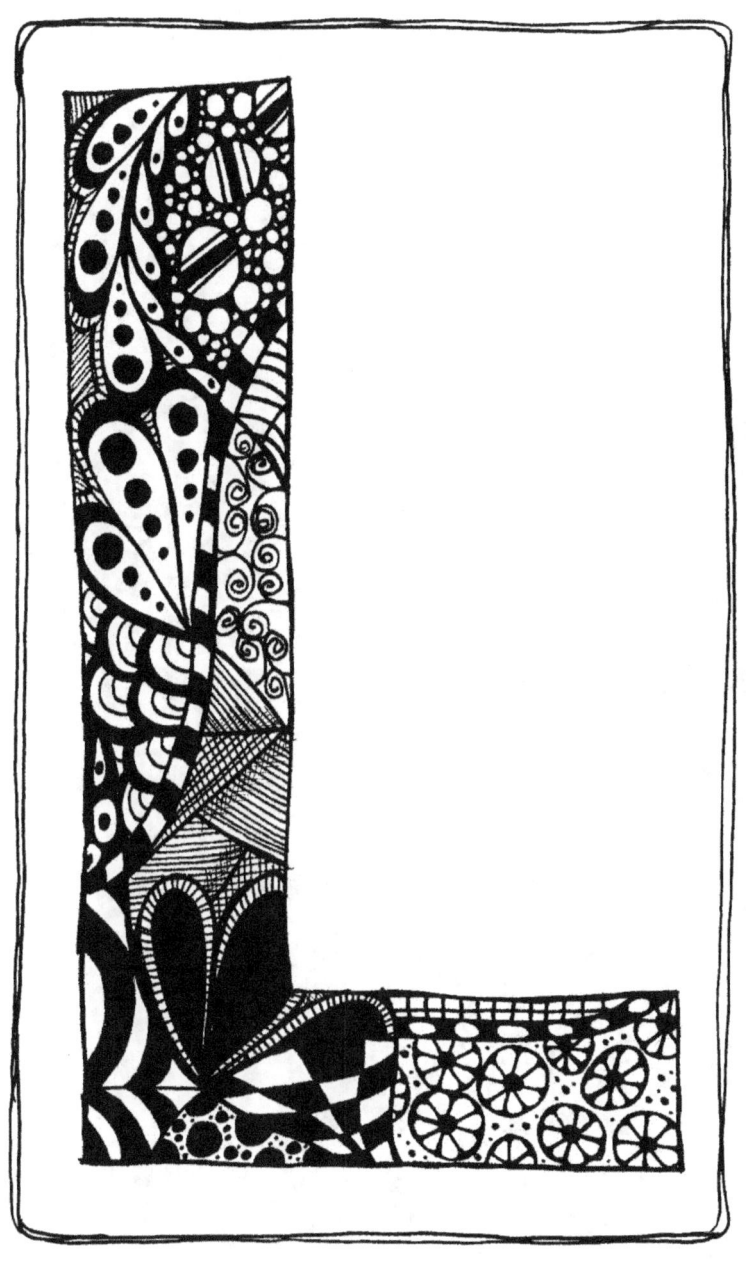

Your letter

Your letter

Your letter

NOTES:

NOTES:

Practice
Here

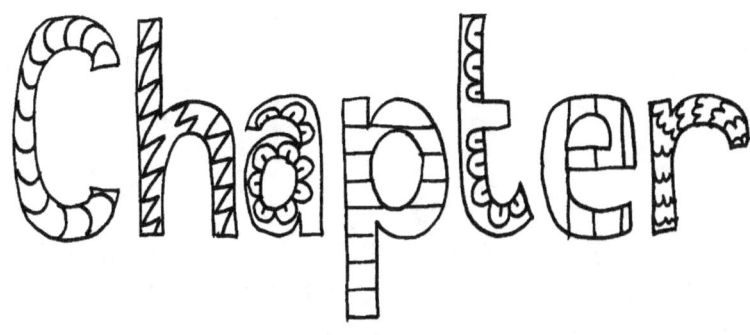

FIVE

MARVELLOUS MACHINES

My fascination with machines was inspired by my all time favourite book and movie, Charlie and the Chocolate Factory. Watching Willy Wonka's amazing machines blew my mind. How did these crazy designs produce such amazing sweets?

What books or movies have inspired you? What marvellous machines have you thought about while reading books? What type of machine might have been used to create those wonderful images?

Juicing Machine

What happens when you want to make an apple juice?

This machine was inspired by the idea of making apple juice in a new and wacky way.

I doubt it would work, but it certainly includes lots of fabulous spinning wheels, pipes, levers, lights, buttons, and other confusing bits and pieces along the way.

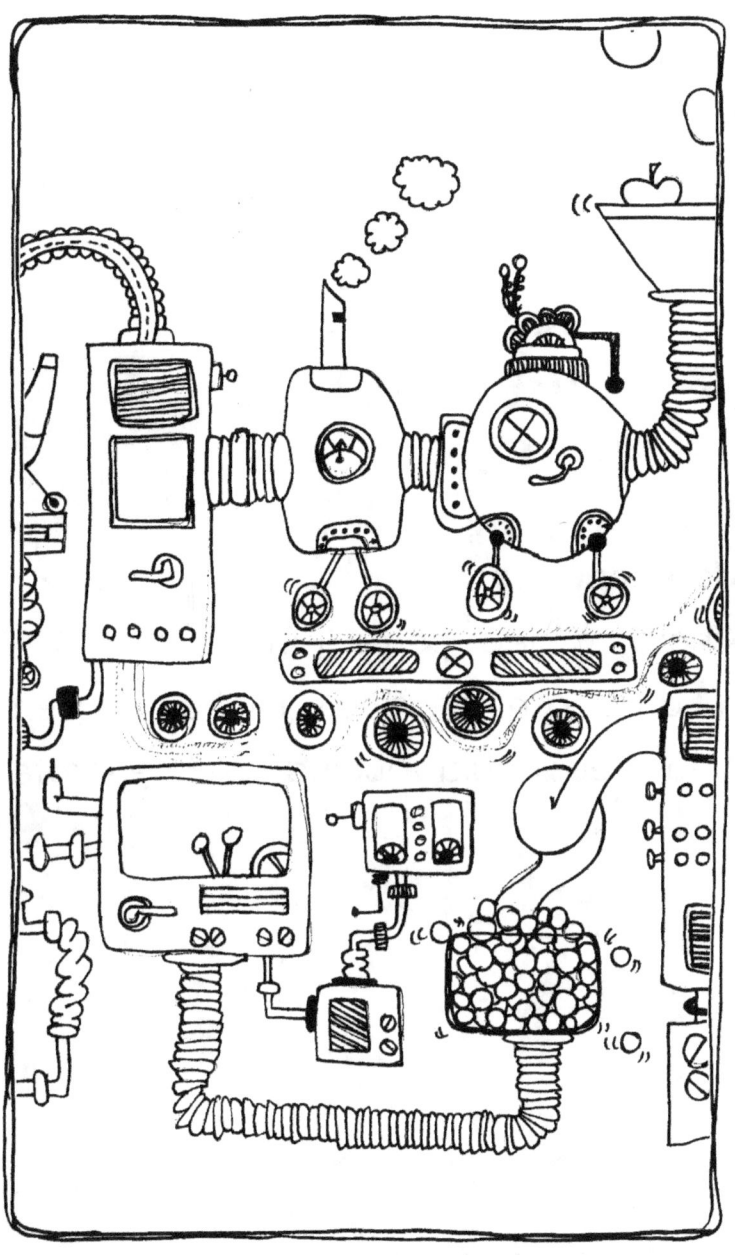

Idea generator

Where do ideas come from?

Put an idea in here and see what happens.

What ideas could your machine generate?

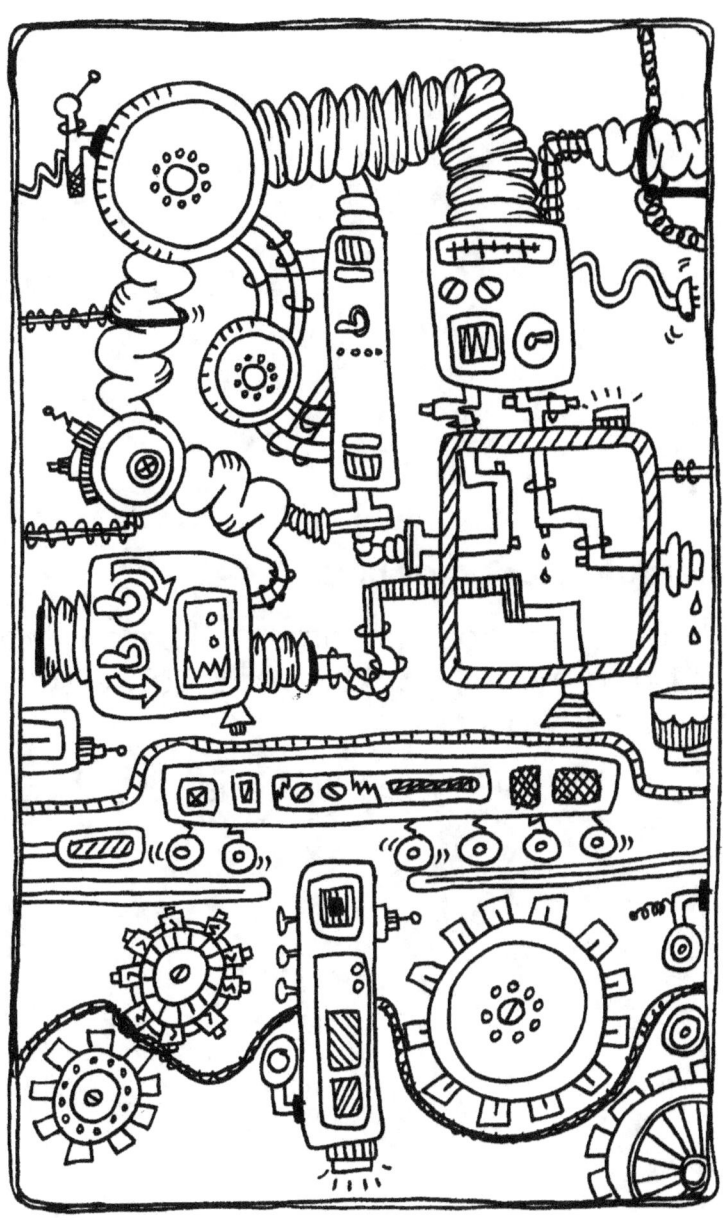

Alternate work machine

What if someone, or something, could do your homework, housework, office work or any other work?

Maybe this machine is the answer.

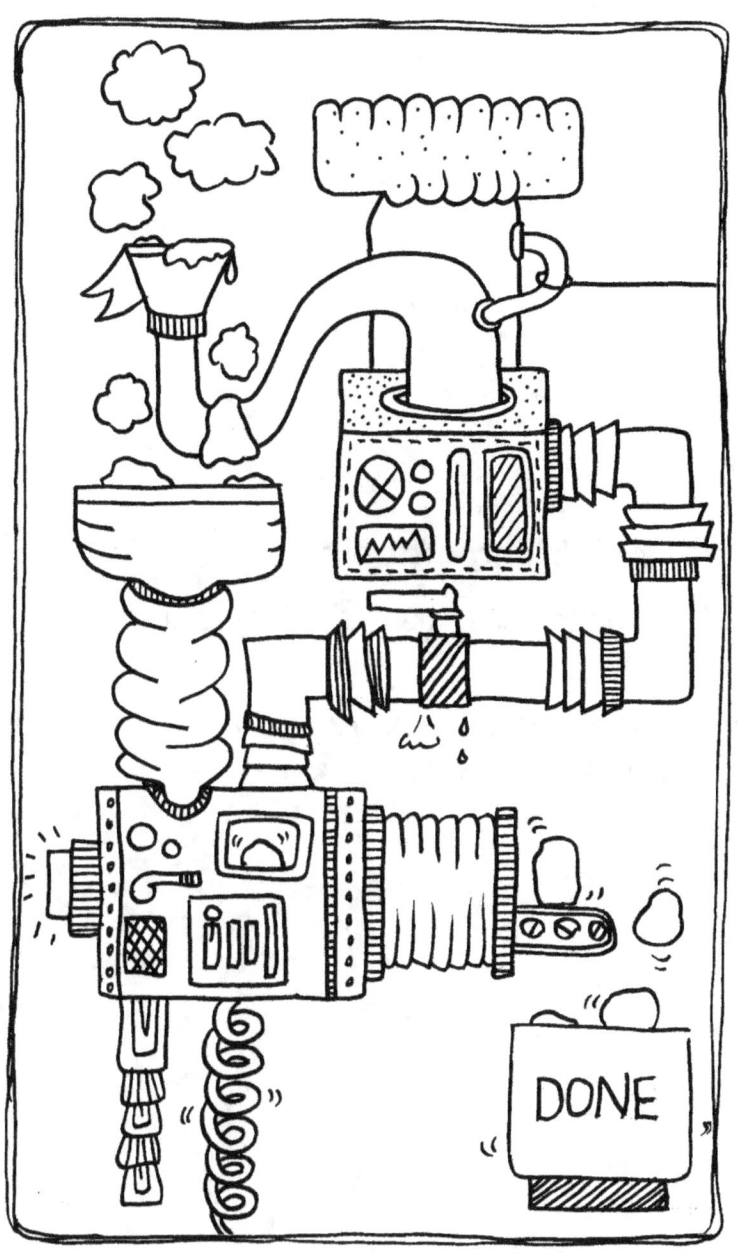

Book publishing machine

Like baking a cake, this machine bakes books.

Inspired by my work in publishing – put in some quality content and out comes a quality book.

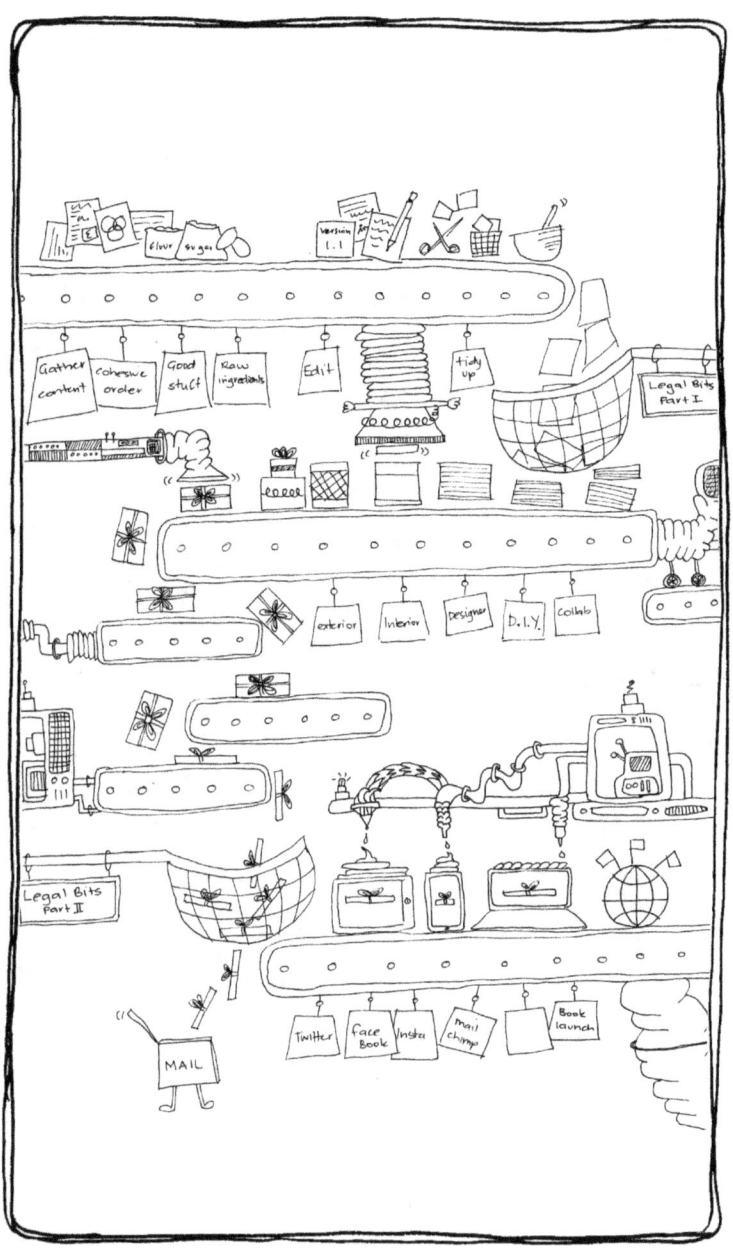

Your machine

Your machine

Your machine

Your machine

NOTES:

NOTES:

More Reading

Colour theory

The focus of this book is to help you create great images in black and white, without worrying about colour.

However, if you'd like to get more into colouring, you may like to explore the science of colour theory.

Betty Edwards's book *Colour* is a great place to start.

She includes information about the history and science of colour theory, as well as emotional effects and combinations.

A colour wheel is also useful for understanding colour. You can purchase a colour wheel online or look at one online.

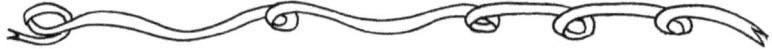

More Resources

Google

Looking on the internet for information about drawing, can overwhelm you with too many resources.

So try refining your search as much as you can, for instance:

City you are interested in

Suburb of the city

Time of day

Perspective

Style

So this could look like:

Brisbane, city, noon, riverside, sketch

While this will still come back with a lot of images, it will give you a much more refined focus.

Skillshare – www.skillshare.com

As the website states, Skillshare is a "learning community for creators".

You can access online tutorials with step-by-step videos showing you how to create great art and improve your skills.

These tutorials can be watched for inspiration or for the love of learning.

Maybe you could even become a tutor!

Instagram

Currently this social media tool is being hailed as the place to go to.

With images being easy to sort, understand and respond to, Instagram has gained a strong foothold in social media.

Follow a few inspiring people to keep your ideas flowing.

As with Google, keep your search word – i.e. hash tag – specific so you can find images that are truly what you are looking for.

YouTube

YouTube has amazing videos compiled by people who are passionate (and patient) about sharing their crafts.

Again define your search well so that you can find what you are actually looking for.

Other resources and inspiration

Joanna Basford
colormecreative.com (Kristina Webb)
Adult Colouring Books
Kikki-K
Just Jaimee
Pinterest
Millie Marcotta

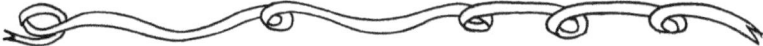

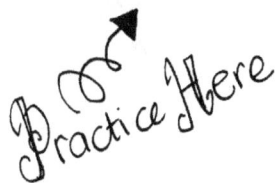

Thank you to you

Thank you to you, reader of this book, dreamer of images, and creator of wonderful patterns.

May you enjoy creating and sharing your tangles.

Practice Here

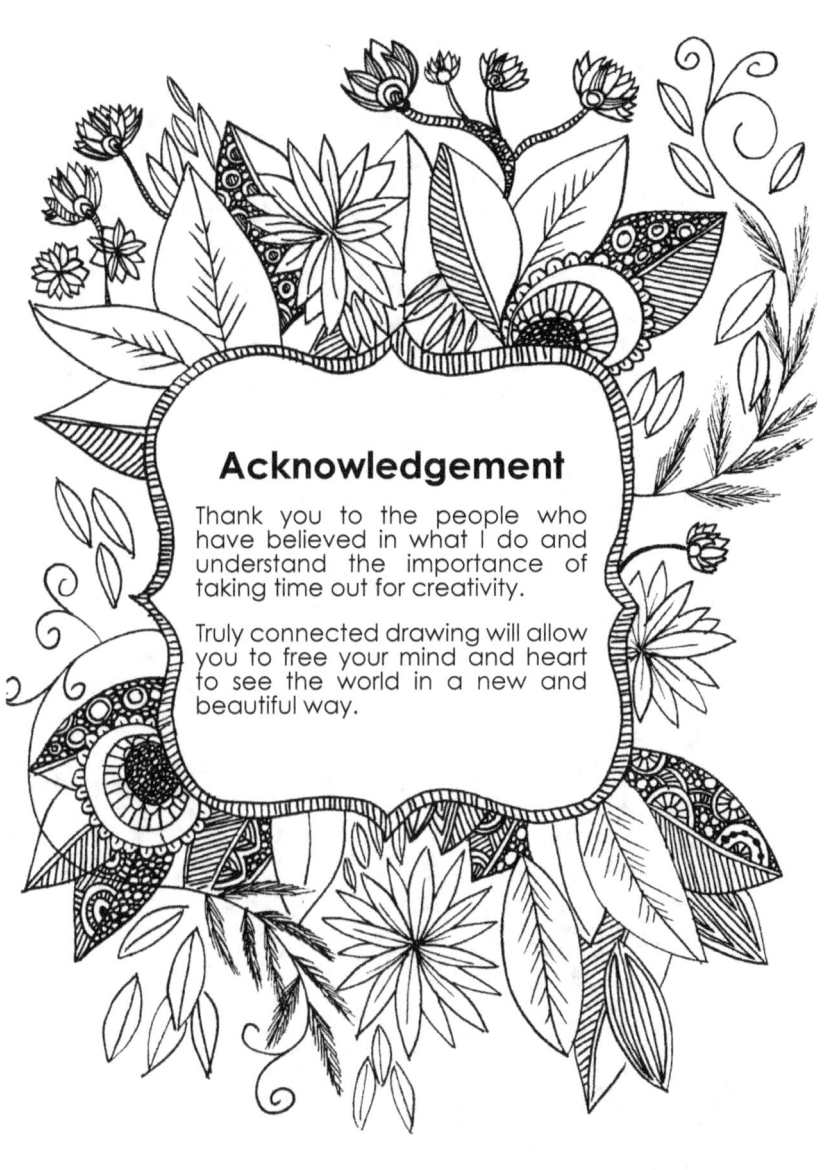

Acknowledgement

Thank you to the people who have believed in what I do and understand the importance of taking time out for creativity.

Truly connected drawing will allow you to free your mind and heart to see the world in a new and beautiful way.

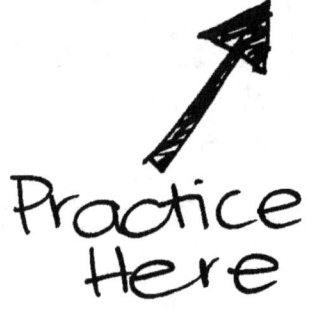

Practice
Here

About the Author

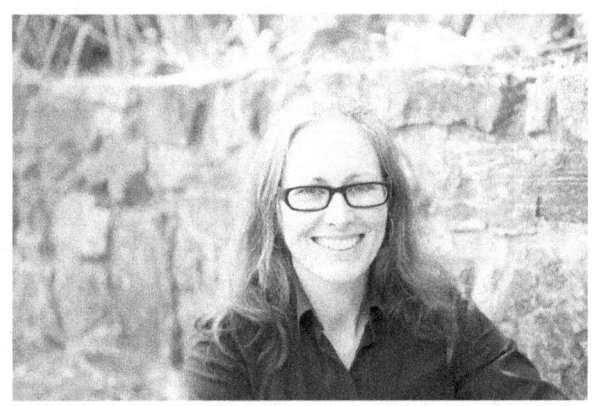

As a country girl beginning life in rural Victoria and NSW, you can imagine the gorgeous surrounds, quirky people and outdoor adventures that dotted the landscape of Dyan's early years. A fascination with people and their vast potential followed her through a science degree, extending into two decades of banking and finance, travel adventures, family creation and business development.

In recent years, Dyan has mastered the field of independent publishing and linked it closely with her passion for organising information, developing effective processes and continuous learning. Her passion for books extends from writing children's manuscripts right through to helping business people to turn their expertise into a published work.

She has always nurtured her creative side and, in recent years, has discovered the joys of creating tangle drawings and visual note taking.

Dyan now carries a notebook and pen wherever she goes, and creates beautiful visual expressions of the world around her, whether drawing a landscape or taking notes at a presentation.

Dyan is now creating several 'how to' guides to inspire others to embrace the joy of drawing, and is regularly commissioned by event organisers to 'draw' the key points of speakers' presentations.

Simply put, Dyan is about getting things done... creatively.

Other titles by Dyan Burgess

Bake a (Business) Book

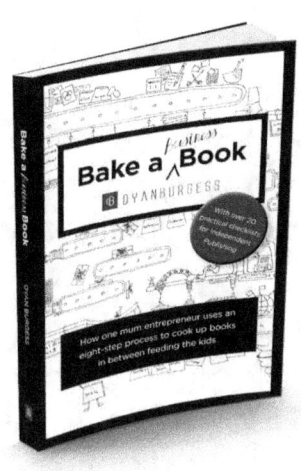

Wanting to publish a book about your expertise? Thought that you don't have the time or the content.

Wanting a business card that has more than your name and email address on it?

What if you handed prospects a book that you published? Would that make a difference to your business?

This book provides an entrepreneur mum's eight-step process to cook up independently published business books in between feeding four kids.

The Visual Note Taking Handbook

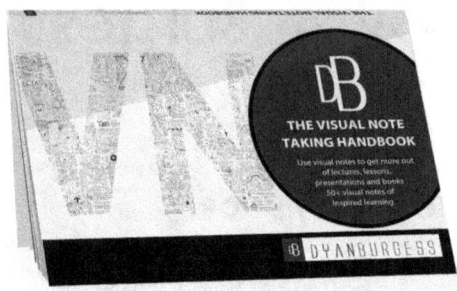

What if you could make listening to lectures, lessons or presentations exciting? What if you took notes in a way that you wanted to review your notes again and again? Sound impossible!

Make it possible using visual note taking techniques. Utilise the collection of over 50 visual notes of inspired learning to assist creating your visual note taking diary.

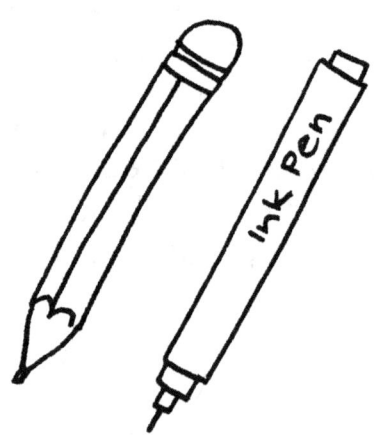

Practice
Here

National Library of Australia Cataloguing-in-Publication entry

Creator: Burgess, Dyan, author, illustrator.

Title: D. I. Y. tangled patterns : step-by-step guide to create
              personalised colouring images / Dyan Burgess.

ISBN: 978-1-925406-28-3 (paperback)

ISBN: 978-1-925406-29-0 (ebook : Kindle)

ISBN: 978-1-925406-30-6 (ebook : ePub)

Subjects: Repetitive patterns (Decorative arts)
              Coloring books.

Other Creators/Contributors: Dedicated Book Services, (www.netdbs.com).

Dewey Number: 741.2

When reviewing could you please mention:

www.dyanburgess.com

While the author has made every effort to provide accurate Internet addresses at the time of publication, neither the author nor the publisher assumes responsibility for errors, or changes that occur after publication. Further, the publisher does not have any control over, and does not assume any responsibility for, author or third-party websites or their content.

Published by D & M Fancy Pastry Pty Ltd in 2016